# Psychoanalysis
# and
# Literature

# Psychoanalysis

# and

# Literature

## An Introduction

Robert N. Mollinger

NELSON-HALL nh CHICAGO

---

---

LIBRARY OF CONGRESS CATALOGING IN PUBLICATION DATA

Mollinger, Robert N    1945–
   Psychoanalysis and literature.

   Bibliography: p.
   Includes index.
   1. American literature—History and criticism.
2. Psychoanalysis and literature.    I. Title.
PS88.M57    810'.9    80-26256
ISBN 0-88229-363-X

Manufactured in the United States of America.

10    9    8    7    6    5    4    3    2    1

*To Shern*

# Contents

# Preface

Since the turn of the century when psychoanalysis began, it has been involved both with literature and with literary criticism. Just as Freud was influenced and inspired by writers such as Dostoevsky and Shakespeare, twentieth-century writers, such as Thomas Mann and Eugene O'Neill, have drawn on Freud's insights in the creation of their works. In their respective searches for meaning — meaning in man's behavior, in his relationships, and in his existence in the world — psychoanalysis and literature have found in each other compatible and comparable humanistic endeavours. Literary critics, seeking thematic meaning and aesthetic unity in literary works, particularly have drawn on the psychoanalytic method for understanding multiple meanings, formal complexities, and the involvement of human personality in the literary experience. It is this relationship between psychoanalysis and literary criticism which I will explore.

My framework for this exploration is broad. I understand psychoanalysis as a developing discipline — one in which some hypotheses are certain, some are yet to be ascertained, and some are questionable. There is a body of knowledge generally agreed upon, and it is this knowledge from which I have most frequently drawn. But there are also theories, not accepted by the mainstream of psychoanalysis, which have attracted much professional and popular attention. For instance, Jung's work not only has been used by analytical psychologists but has particularly attracted literary critics. Although Jungian theories have not been integrated into the commonly accepted framework of psychoanalysis (at some point they may be), I have included an application of Jungian ideas to literature because it is a common critical approach to literature. Similarly, I have illustrated differing psychoanalytic approaches to literature: those which concern author, art work, and audience. These approaches have not been integrated into a coherent whole. Since both man's personality and man's literature are complex, differing psychoanalytic and critical theories must be explored, and taken seriously, if they do shed light on their respective subjects. In time, psychoanalytic knowledge may be more integrated, and literary criticism may be more unified; for now, it is best to remain aware of a broad framework for both. This being so, in *Psychoanalysis and Literature: An Introduction* I introduce the reader to this interdisciplinary field and illustrate various kinds of psychoanalytic approaches to literature.

From this perspective Chapter One reviews ways psychoanalysis has been applied to the literary author, the literary work, and the reader of literature. In Chapter Two I provide an introduction to psychoanalytic theory, clinical data, and a survey of the development of the personality. Chapters Three through Eleven illustrate how such psychoanalytic knowledge can be used in literary criticism.

In Chapter Three, exploring the meaning of a literary symbol, I apply Jung's concept of the archetypal hero to the symbolism of Wallace Stevens's image of the hero. In Chapter Four, which examines the personality of a literary character, I use the psychoanalyst's knowledge of depression to understand Edgar Allan Poe's Roderick Usher in "The Fall of the House of Usher." In Chapter Five, describing the unity of a literary work, I focus on the oral imagery of Herman Melville's "Bartleby the Scrivener." Chapters Six, Seven, and Eight explore the literary oeuvre as a whole. In them, I examine father symbolism in Sylvia Plath's poetry, the relation of psychic merger to form and content in Dom Moraes's works, and the oedipus complex and philosophic naturalism in Wallace Stevens's poetry. Chapters Nine and Ten explore Wallace Stevens's adolescence and adulthood and Edgar Allan Poe's infancy and childhood and attempt to show the relationship of an author's life to his work. Finally, in Chapter Eleven, I turn to the reader of literature and argue that the reader's personality affects his literary preferences.

As it is with any book, many people have been especially helpful. First and foremost among these has been my wife, Shernaz Mollinger, who has read several complete drafts and whose comments have improved both its arguments and its style; to her, I am most indebted and grateful. I particularly thank Dr. Bertram Kirsch who commented on Chapter Two. His help throughout the past several years has greatly increased my understanding of psychoanalysis and of people. Likewise, for aiding in my understanding of psychoanalysis, I thank Dr. Herb Freudenberger and the late Adolf G. Woltmann. Mentors from the past who influenced the present and to whom I am and will always remain grateful are Professors Norman S. Care and Robert E. Gross. Without the past influence of my parents, Owen and Florence, I would not have had the discipline and perseverance necessary to complete this book. Finally, I am indebted to Nassau Community College which provided me with a sabbatical to complete this project and to the National Psychological Association for Psychoanalysis which trained me in psychoanalysis.

# Acknowledgments

Several chapters of this book are revisions of articles previously published in journals. I would like to thank the editors of those journals for their permission to reprint the following:

Ch. 3: Originally published as "Hero as Poetic Image," *Psychological Perspectives*, 5, no. 1 (Spring 1974), pp. 60–66.

Ch. 6: Originally published as "A Symbolic Complex: Images of Death and Daddy in the Poetry of Sylvia Plath," *Descant*, 19, no. 2 (Winter 1975), pp. 44–52.

Ch. 7: Originally published as "Psychic Images and Poetic Technique in Dom Moraes' Poetry," *World Literature Written in English*, 14, no. 2 (November, 1975), pp. 322–28.

# 1

# A Review
# of Psychoanalytic
# Literary Criticism

In 1895, Sigmund Freud, with Joseph Breuer, published *Studies in Hysteria*. This showed how some hysterical symptoms, such as pain and paralyses, are caused by ideas — ideas which because they are inadmissible to consciousness become pathogenic. In 1900, Freud, alone, published *The Interpretation of Dreams*. It outlined a complete theory of dreams and focused on unconscious mechanisms and their relation to consciousness. Psychoanalysis was born. Soon after, in addition to developing psychoanalysis as a discipline in its own right, Freud began to apply it to other fields of inquiry. In 1905 (*Jokes and Their Relation to the Unconscious*), he attempted to understand wit psychoanalytically. By 1907, in *Delusions and Dreams in Jensen's Gradiva*, which psychoanalyzes the delusions and dreams of a literary character Norbert Hanold, he was already developing the field of psychoanalytic literary criticism he had started in *The Interpretation of Dreams* with his examination of Sophocles' *Oedipus Rex* and Shakespeare's *Hamlet* for their oedipal elements and for the effects the plays had on their audience. "Creative Writers and Day-dreaming" delivered as a lecture in 1907 and published in 1908 further expands the connection between literature and psychoanalysis. It compares fantasy, play, dreams, and the work of art in order to understand creativity. In 1910, Freud examined the life of Leonardo da Vinci and linked his paintings to it. Though not a study of a literary figure, this book, as a work of applied psychoanalysis, completed the parameters Freud developed for applied psychoanalysis. Psychoanalysis contributes to an understanding of the art work (the literary piece itself including the characters in it), the artist (writer including his creative process), and the audience (readers and their responses).

### Psychoanalytic Theories of Literature

"Creative Writers and Day-dreaming," contained Freud's first theory on the structure of the literary work and began the psychoanalytic enquiry into what literature is. For Freud, literature, a novel for example, was analogous to a daydream. Like a daydream, the literary piece contains in its phantasy the fulfillment of an unsatisfied wish and thus improves on an unsatisfactory reality:

> The fact that all women in the novel invariably fall in love with the hero can hardly be looked on as a portrayal of reality, but it is easily understood as a necessary constituent of a daydream. (p. 150)

Though Freud mentions that he is only speaking of the works of "less pretentious authors." in fact, he generalized the wish-fulfilling element of the creative product to all authors. The content is a phantasy of fulfillment, whereas the formal elements of the work are meant to disguise the wish, since fulfillment of the wish is overtly repulsive or unacceptable to the writer: "the essential *ars poetica* lies in the technique of overcoming the feeling of repulsion. . . . The writer softens the character of his egoistic day-dreams by altering and disguising it. . . ." (p. 153). In this essay Freud lays down the basic perspective that psychoanalysts have continued to take on literature: literature satisfies unfulfilled, partially unacceptable and therefore unconscious wishes in a disguised fashion.

In fact, literature is like a dream. The literary work has symbols which must be understood, and according to Freud psychoanalysis can unravel the meaning of the symbols. In "The Theme of the Three Caskets" (1913), Freud argues that the caskets in Shakespeare's *The Merchant of Venice* represent the mother in three forms — mother herself, wife, and mother earth. His method of explication uses myths, dreams, dream mechanisms (for example, reversal), and references to other literary works to arrive at the "original meaning."

Following Freud's ideas, critics soon made his basic insights explicit. Wilhelm Stekel (1923) holds that "there is essentially no difference between dream and poetry," and F. C. Prescott, especially in *Poetry and Dreams* (1912), attempts to document their relationship extensively both in form and content (see Morrison, 1968, on Prescott). But though Prescott in his later work does attempt to move beyond the unconscious elements in the literary piece, not until Ernst Kris, in *Psychoanalytic Explorations in Art* (1952), were elements besides the unconscious fantasy systematically focused on by a sophisticated psychoanalyst. Kris still holds to the idea that the dream and art can be compared: "What in the dream appears as compromise and is explained in terms of overdetermination appears in the work of art as multiplicity of meaning. . . ." This is a comparison which is important, according to Kris, because of their differences. In dreams, the id, the reservoir of impulses and wishes, is in control; however, in the art work it is the ego, the organizing function of the psyche, which is in control. The primary process, how the unconscious functions (condensation, displacement), may be contained in a work, but the process is in the service of the ego, that is, it is under control. Thus, to understand meaning in literature, as well as to interpret symbols, one must be aware that the unconscious meaning will not be the only meaning:

> The meaning of a symbol word varies according to the context in which it is construed. . . . One cannot speak, therefore, of *the* meaning of any symbol, but can only specify its range of responses and the clusters into which these tend to be grouped.

> We refer to this general characteristic of language as *ambigu-
> ity*. (pp. 244–45)

Though emphasizing that much of the ambiguity comes from
the work of the primary process, Kris implies that some comes
from higher cognitive functioning as well. "No account of the
aesthetic process can be adequate without giving due weight
to this 'intellectual' component" (p. 254).

Further, for Kris, the dream is an intrapsychic process,
while art is an interpersonal one. He says, "Wherever artistic
creation takes place, the idea of a public exists" (p. 60). Art not
only contains the satisfaction of unacceptable wishes but is
also an act of communication." Art . . . always, consciously
or unconsciously, serves the purpose of communication" (p.
61). The focus again moves from the unconscious wish to the
controlling ego, the ways and modes of communication, and
analysis of style and formal elements in literature becomes
necessary. Ambiguity in poetry, as well as in other arts, is seen
as communicating a multiplicity of meanings to the reader;
metaphor is seen in a similar way.

Besides his focus on the formal elements of art, Kris points
to another area, the reality in which the artist creates:

> The structure of the problem which exists while the artist is
> creating, the historical circumstances in the development of
> art itself which limit some of his work, determine in one way
> or another his mode of expression and thus constitute the stuff
> with which he struggles in creation. (p. 15)

Having gone beyond the id to the ego, beyond the content to
the form, beyond the intrapsychic to the interpersonal, Kris
here implies the need to go beyond the personal to the social,
perhaps even to the psychohistorical.

Norman Holland (1968) continues Kris's interest in the
multitudinal aspects of the literary work and attempts to create a theory of literature which will explain fully both the
content and the form. Defining meaning as "an idea that all
the particular details of a work are 'about,' " he distinguishes
two levels:

> The first, conventional literary meaning, states the way the elements of the story are relevant to an intellectual idea. . . . The second, a psychoanalytic statement, shows how the elements of the story, understood as having unconscious meanings, . . . are all relevant to a particular unconscious fantasy. . . . (p. 12)

Literary meaning is seen as a transformation of an unconscious fantasy into social, moral, intellectual, and mythic terms which are understood by, and relevant to, the conscious mind. Holland is here elaborating on Freud's earlier emphasis on fantasy, especially unconscious fantasy, as the essential aspect of the literary work: "the psychoanalytic meaning underlies all the others" (p. 27; see also Lesser, 1957).

Defining form as "the ordering and structuring of parts," Holland explains it as a defense against the unconscious fantasy. Since the unconscious fantasy is threatening and dangerous, formal elements are used to make it pleasurable — by making it relevant to the conscious intellect. Since form adapts the unconscious meaning to the more acceptable intellectual meaning, it is progressive, a movement forward, as well as defensive. The ways form accomplishes this are manifold. For instance, fantasy which might be upsetting is put into words that help to master, control, and dilute its emotional element. The sound of words also provides a physical way of dealing with content. In general, "form can only be understood as managing fantasy content" (p. 157). Holland has developed a theory of literature based on the psychoanalytic theory of the structure of the mind. Since impulses or wishes seek satisfaction (the id) but are opposed by values the mind holds essential (the superego), these wishes must be molded into a compromise form (by the ego).

Another recent psychoanalytic approach to literature also focuses primarily on the unconscious. Critics influenced by Lacan (1966) seek to find the language of the unconscious in the language of literature for "*the structure of the unconscious is the structure of language*" (Miel, 1965, p. 98). A literary interpretation from this perspective focuses on the details of the literary text in order to establish a coherent, metaphoric sequence in the text which reflects an unconscious fantasy (Doubrovsky, 1978, p. 317).

Holland's theory and Lacanian criticism are predominantly based on the psychoanalytic theory of conflicts within the psyche. Recently, however, psychoanalysis has begun to include theories concerning the interactions between the child and mother. Some psychoanalytic theories of literature are now beginning to deem this interpersonal aspect of human psychological development important to art. British psychoanalyst D. W. Winnicott (1951) postulates there is an intermediate area of experience, transitional space, between inner reality (the subjective) and external reality (the objective). An infant at first has no conception of the external or of another person; all experience is *his* experience. Eventually he will realize that external reality and other people, starting with his mother, exist in their own right, but this occurs slowly. On his way to this realization, he invests objects such as teddy bears and blankets, provided by external reality with his own illusions. For instance, he believes that he created the object and that it is symbolic of something, like the maternal breast. However, this object, the "transitional object," importantly partakes of both the internal and the external:

> It is true that the piece of blanket (or whatever it is) is symbolical of some part-object, such as the breast. Nevertheless, the point of it is not its symbolic value so much as its actuality. Its not being the breast (or the mother), although real, is as important as the fact that it stands for the breast (or the mother). (Winnicott, 1951, p. 233)

The transitional object is material provided by the environment (the mother) and molded by the infant with illusion, and Winnicott (1967) compares this to culture, in our terms cultural products such as literature: "The place where cultural experience is located is in the *potential space* between the individual and the environment (originally the object)" (p. 101). The creative product, the literary work, can be seen as the interpenetration of the artist's self, his creative illusion, and the environment, the material. This material can be both the art medium (words and the forms they are put in) and tradition (the previous history of the use of words in novels, poems and plays). As Modell (1970) puts it, "culture, which is the creative transformation of the environment, bears the imprint of the psychological equation, mother = environment" (p. 249). Whereas Freud and Holland would hold that the literary work is the externalization of an intra-psychic conflict, this theory emphasizes the relation of art to the interaction between self and other.

## CRITICISMS OF PSYCHOANALYTIC THEORIES OF LITERATURE

Numerous criticisms have been voiced ever since psycho-analysis began being applied to literature. Some of these are to the point; others are not. For instance, it has been held that psychoanalytic literary criticism is full of mechanical jargon. Kazin (1959) believes it has become pedantic and unrelated to living literature. Crews (1970) directly attacks Holland's work on this account:

> A criticism that cheerfully catalogs the unconscious tricks we play on ourselves and equates literary power with a judicious recipe of wishes and tactics, introjection and intellection, cannot avoid becoming a new version of anaesthetics. . . . (p. 19)

Though there may be legitimate points of criticism implied here, stress on the mechanical approach and the terminology being used is not one of them. Griffin (1951), in opposition, clearly states the obvious: "It is reasonable to expect a new science to develop terminology indispensable to the application of its concepts" (p. 22). As psychoanalysis develops, more precise terminology is being used. In addition, attempts are now being made to revise psychoanalytic terminology as a whole (Schafer, 1976). To reject a discipline because of its terminology is to confuse what is central and what is accidental.

Other criticisms of the methods of psychoanalytic literary criticism deplore its frequently limited focus. For instance, we have seen in Freud's and Holland's works that psychoanalysis can show the interrelations of the parts of the literary work. Slochower (1971), a practicing psychoanalytic literary critic himself, suggests that in analyzing the content of the work alone, the affect in art as conveyed by its formal elements is ignored. Though this may at times be true, there is much significant work which does analyze form. For instance, Holland, as we have seen, has emphasized the defensive function of language, sound, and metaphor. With regard to drama, he puts his focus in clear perspective, "consider . . . the formal interrelations between the various parts of the play, the wholeness of it, and this is what the 'newer' kind of psychoanalytic criticism has begun to do." (Holland, 1962, p. 221). Schwartz (1973) feels that traditional psychoanalytic criticism has objectified the literary text and fails to recognize the subjective element involved. We shall see later how Holland (1975a) has attempted to take this element into account. Winnicott (1971) also has recognized this problem, "To some extent objectivity is a relative term because what is objectively perceived is by definition to some extent subjectively conceived of" (p. 66). We shall see later how the role of subjectivity has become of essential importance in the views of many critics.

The criticisms reviewed have been mainly by practicing psychoanalytic literary critics themselves — showing that the field is vital and changing. Essentially, these criticisms are all related to the most popular criticism, the one that has hounded psychoanalysis since its origin: psychoanalysis reduces the meaning of acts and, more importantly in our context, the meaning of the literary work to the "one, true meaning." It is illegitimately reductionist. Slochower (1971) complains about too much emphasis on content, Schwartz (1973) of too much on objectivity, and Burke (1939) says that psychoanalysis is "essentializing." Trilling (1940) objects that "there is no single meaning to any work of art." A variant of this criticism by Crews (1975) is that there is too much emphasis on the infantile elements in psychoanalytic literary

criticism. He develops this idea extensively: the way psychoanalysis itself approaches interpretations of acts dictates reductionism. Psychoanalysis reduces everything to conflict, and all
new psychoanalytic theorizing, as for instance Winnicott's, is
still reductionist. However Crews himself provides us with an
answer to such criticisms: "the mere proposing of a reductive
idea doesn't in itself constitute reduction*ism*, the effective denial or denigration of all meanings but the reductive one that
is being revealed. . . . Reductionism proper is a certain big-
oted way of advancing such points, with the result that the
work in its singularity is sacrificed to the interpretive scheme
instead of being illuminated by it" (p. 545). The distinction is
well put and should be well taken. One can make a psychoanalytic statement about a literary text without negating
others (for instance, Roland and Rizzo, 1977, and Mollinger,
R. and Mollinger, S., 1979). There are some other consider-
ations, however.

First, all literary criticism, not just psychoanalytic criticism, *reduces* meanings to one meaning; it is a way of writing,
a way of debating, a way of putting a point. Crews (1966)
himself in writing about Nathaniel Hawthorne's later ro-
mances says:

> But exactly the same Oedipal situations, the same images, the
> same fears, the same dynamics of repression and expression are
> discernible in Hawthorne's most polished and powerful work.
> *Must we not conclude* that he is an obsessed writer throughout
> his career, and that the differences from one phase to another
> are finally differences in self-control rather than in energy or
> ideas. (p. 257; my italics)

Apparently, we must, but critics who "stick to the text" write
the same way. In opposing another critic's contention about a
poem by Emily Dickinson, Henry (1973) asserts "Bona-fide
poet that she is, Miss Dickinson would scorn the device of
creating disturbance in her reader by bewildering him with
grammatical hurdles." Apparently we must agree with Henry
because if we interpret any other way we do not know a

"bona-fide" poet from a false one. The important point here is that it would be the psychoanalytic critic who would be accused of reductionism, not the other, even though most critics state their point, *as a matter of style*, in the most forceful way possible.

Second, the reductionist argument frequently holds that psychoanalysis always finds castration anxiety and the primal scene in literature. This may have been true at one time, but the reasons for this have been obscured. On the one hand, psychoanalysis as a science first focused on oedipal conflicts; other areas of psychological concern were not yet noted. One cannot apply what one does not know. As the field expanded, new theories, as those of earlier developmental concerns, were postulated. In the past, hysterical symptoms were always viewed in relation to oedipal conflicts; it is now realized that they may be connected to earlier developmental stages. Literary critics are in a position to apply this new knowledge as well as psychoanalysts. Noland (1973), for example, has proposed that Erik Erikson's epigenetic schema for the understanding of psychological development throughout life be applied in literary studies. On the other hand, though psychoanalytic knowledge may have been limited earlier, some practitioners of psychoanalytic criticism have always been aware only of specific areas of psychoanalysis and have thus produced limited work. Crews, who was extremely well versed in psychoanalysis for a professor of literature, emphasized incest in his study of Hawthorne in 1966; yet well before then preoedipal concerns of the child had been studied and hypothesized.

Finally, even if Crews shows us only the oedipal manifestations in Hawthorne's work, it is difficult to see the harm in this. It may be a limited insight, but it is an insight; in all likelihood, another critic will expand our knowledge of Hawthorne by explaining other aspects of the literary work in question. To state the obvious: one man cannot do it all. Just as Freud's insights are developed and expanded, the particular insights of individual critics will be developed and expanded. As Meissner (1973) puts it, "it must be remembered that division does not necessarily mean separation. . . . There is a validity and pertinence to each of the levels of analysis — regardless of the meaningful patterns of integration and mutual interaction" they may enjoy among themselves" (p. 262). A deep examination of oedipal elements by one critic allows us to understand those elements in a literary work. This does not mean that those elements are separate from others. Their relevance to other elements may be examined by another critic later, just as an extensive analysis of the sound pattern of a poem by one critic can later be related by another critic to the metaphors in the poem.

### THE PSYCHOANALYTIC STUDY OF CHARACTER

Related to the psychoanalytic study of the literary work itself is the interpretation of particular characters who appear in novels and plays. As we have seen earlier, Freud (1900) begins this kind of enquiry in his remarks on Hamlet. Ernest Jones (1955) further extends this approach. He begins by focusing on the main obscurity of Shakespeare's *Hamlet* — why does Hamlet delay in killing Claudius even though he believes Claudius murdered his father? Finding other explanations inadequate, Jones hypothesizes that Hamlet has incestuous desires for his mother and death wishes for his father. When Claudius commits incest with Hamlet's mother, Gertrude, Hamlet identifies with him because of his own similar wishes; to kill Claudius means for Hamlet to kill himself. In addition, Claudius has replaced Hamlet's father and has thus symbolically become Hamlet's father; to kill Claudius also means to kill the father and to commit patricide. For Jones, this complexity of feeling explains Hamlet's hesitancy to act, and he then attempts to understand Hamlet's other interactions in the play, with Polonius and with Ophelia, in the light of Hamlet's conflicts. As we have seen, the psychoanalytic literary critic studies the literary character as a psychoanalyst studies a patient (Meissner, 1973) — there is a search for patterns of behavior, unconscious motivations, and, in general, the typical way the person relates to himself and others.

CRITICISMS

There have been two main objections to this kind of approach. First, the characters in literature are not living people, and therefore psychoanalysis cannot study them. Slochower (1971) says, "Art deals with human experience; but it does so in its symbolic forms. Hence, to treat characters in literature as living people is to confuse the esthetic and symbolic with the factual and the existent" (p. 109). Slochower here misses the point that in art we arrive at the human experience partially because its characters are representations of the human — either types, particular emotions, or conflicts. As Meissner (1973) puts it, "To say, for example, that a character is fictional need not imply that the character is thereby distorted or unreal. In fact, the literary character can have a quality of integration and human substance which makes the character as real to our understanding as that of any human person" (p. 266). A further problem with this criticism is that all literary critics, not psychoanalytic ones only, have studied characters in literature. Jones (1955) points out how Goethe saw Hamlet as "oversensitive" and how Coleridge thought Hamlet had an "overbalance in the contemplative faculty." The question is not whether characters will be interpreted psychologically but with what means we shall go about doing it. Shall we use popular every-day psychology and think we are making significant statements, or shall we use the most sophisticated theory of personality we have, psychoanalysis? Daiches (1965) pointedly sums up the advantages of the latter choice. If literature illuminates the human situation, then a psychology of human behavior may provide a pattern for a character's actions and thus a pattern by which to understand the whole work (pp. 349–55). Agreeing with this basic assumption, Noland (1973) suggests using Erikson's theories here as well — examine the character in his personal, developmental context and in the historical context of the community in which he exists (p. 100).

The second criticism of a psychoanalytic interpretation of characters objects to the hypothesis of a past life to the character. For instance, Jones (1955) says, "As a child Hamlet had experienced the warmest affection for his mother, and this, as is always so, had contained elements of a disguised erotic quality, still more so in infancy" (p. 91). Using textual evidence, he shows that the Queen, Hamlet's mother, had a sensual nature in the time period in which the drama takes place; nevertheless, it is impossible to prove she was the same with Hamlet when he was young. Griffin (1951) objects to this tendency to create a past for a character that the author does not supply. This criticism focuses on the essential point: no psychoanalytic interpretation of a literary character can be foolproof. While the psychoanalytic critic may understand the character's contemporary pattern of behavior as given in the text, the critic has no way of testing his hypotheses. In the treatment of a living person, hypotheses regarding the person are constantly refined through new information as treatment progresses. This kind of refinement is unavailable to the literary critic. In treatment, hypotheses about the person's past are continually changed and improved until sufficient accuracy is reached. This is impossible by the nature of a literary character's past. This does not mean that the application of psychoanalysis here is illegitimate, rather we should see this problem in terms of a continuum. At one end we approach accuracy and, at the other, mere speculation. As long as it is kept in mind that speculation is merely speculation about a character's past life, we can hypothesize within reason about that character's present, and hope that this will elucidate the character and the literary work as a whole.

## PSYCHOANALYSIS AND THE WRITER

For psychoanalysis, it has been a short step from the creative product, the literary work, to the creative artist, the maker of literature. In "Creative Writers and Day-

dreaming," Freud suggests that we could study "the connections that exist between the life of the writer and his works" (p.
151). This study has been split into two basic areas: the study
of the creative process of authors in general and the examination of the relation of the psychology of a particular author to
his particular work.

### THE CREATIVE PROCESS

In stating that the literary work is like a daydream, Freud
also hypothesizes about the way literary creation occurs. In
daydreaming, the psyche is stimulated by a current impression which arouses a significant wish; an ensuing fantasy then
fulfills that wish. In creativity,

> A strong experience in the present awakens in the creative
> writer a memory of an earlier experience (usually belonging to
> his childhood) from which there now proceeds a wish which
> finds its fulfillment in the creative work. The work exhibits
> elements of the recent provoking occasion as well as of the old
> memory. (p. 151)

To be an artist then one must have the capability to tap the
unconscious for early experiences easily. Repression, which
makes unacceptable urges unconscious, must be flexible to
allow this. This theory is similar to Freud's dream theory: a
daily event stimulates a childhood wish which is then fulfilled
in the dream. Creating, then, is like dreaming, and like
dreaming it is seen as a solution to a conflict. An unsatisfied
wish is one that has been found unacceptable, and it must
therefore be satisfied in a disguised way, in a dream or as a
work of literature.

Kris (1953) attempts to move away from Freud's emphasis
on the unsatisfied wish arising from the unconscious. For
Freud, art is marked by the primary process mechanisms of
the unconscious, condensation and displacement, and by the
lack of control of the artist himself. For Kris, the creative
process occurs in two steps: inspiration and elaboration. Inspiration is the feeling of being driven and of rapture —
impulses and drives, otherwise hidden, emerge. Elaboration

is the experience of purposeful organization and is characterized by dedication and concentration. Whereas Freud emphasizes psychic conflict, the focus of Kris goes beyond conflict:

> *It seems that in every process of creation the gradual emer-*
> *gence from conflict plays its part.* It may start out in serving a
> fantasy of the individual, in meeting an individual's needs, but
> to the extent that it emerges from conflict, certain properties
> may be acquired which are akin to, and some of them identical
> with gift or skill. We have mentioned that themes may be
> generalized, the emotive potential may grow and the process
> of creative communication may be initiated. All that is not
> only the result of conflict; it is at least in part due to the
> integrative, and in this instance autonomous powers of the
> Ego. (p. 351, Kris's italics)

Kris here begins to take artistic creation out of conflict and
into a nonconflictual area of experience, from the unconscious
and determined area into that of the preconscious (elements
not recognizably conscious but not rejected as unacceptable),
and from there into the area of the conscious and purposeful.
Any regression to primary process thinking is in the service of
the ego (the organizing function of the psyche) and thus is
controlled. The artistic process, then, becomes for Kris (1952)
one of "continual interplay between creation and criticism."
There is "a *shift in psychic level*, consisting in the fluctuation
of functional regression and control" (pp. 253–54).

Freud and Kris have set the parameters for the psychoanalytic study of creativity: exploration of unconscious motivations and exploration of the preconscious. For instance,
Weissman (1968) connects the infantile capacity to halluci-
nate the mother's breast even when not in need of it to the
future artist's ability to elaborate self-created perceptions.
Holland, having developed to its most comprehensive state
the conflict theory of literature, believes that it is the conflict
itself (the unconscious fantasy and its rejection) and the way
the author handles conflict which is reflected in literature. In
his *Poems in Persons* (1973) he seeks "the common source in

childhood of H.D.'s [the poet, Hilda Doolittle] lifestyle and her literary style." Attempting to focus on more than the id, he tries to explain the *way* she handled the conflicting forces acting on her. *"To close the gaps with signs* — this is H.D.'s 'myth' or 'ego identity' or character or 'identity theme,' the style with which her ego mediates among the forces acting on it. We have seen it pervade all her writing and all that we know of her adult life" (p. 51). Although Holland seems to be looking beyond the id, he still emphasizes it, "the psychosexual mode that dominated H.D.'s psyche" (p. 51), and emphasizes, as well, the defensive functions of the ego only, not the adaptive, progressive ones.

Others have followed Kris's lead into the preconscious and conscious more forcefully. Kubie (1958) hypothesizes that the preconscious system is "the essential implement of all creative activity" (p. 137). Both conscious and unconscious symbols are rigid and disrupt the creative preconscious. For Kubie, creativity is "the capacity to find new and unexpected connections" (p. 141) and it is the preconscious, on the fringe of consciousness and unencumbered by the repressed elements in the unconscious, which has the mobility to achieve this. This is because unconscious elements have been kept out of consciousness forcefully due to their unacceptability, while preconscious ones are not rejected nor kept out of consciousness.

Rothenberg (1976) further develops those elements of creativity which are not dependent on the unconscious. For him, what is important is the transformation factor — what makes art out of the unconscious elements. He postulates two kinds of thinking processes, both of them intentional, which artists use in creation. The first, Janusian thinking, "consists of *actively conceiving two or more opposite, contradictory, or antithetical concepts, images, or ideas simultaneously*" (Rothenberg's italics, p. 18). The second, homospatial thinking, "consists of *actively conceiving two or more discrete entities* occupying the same space, a conception leading to *the articulation of new identities*" (p. 18, Rothenberg's italics).

These processes are secondary, not primary ones, and they are adaptive, not regressive. For instance, homospatial thinking can uncover unconscious meaning and produce insight. In contrast, a primary process, like condensation (where a single element in a dream may represent numerous thoughts), distorts and hides unconscious meanings. In dreams, the integration is not clear; in art, it is. Here again we see stress on the nonconscious, the purposeful, and the adaptive.

Arieti (1976) also concentrates on these areas of creativity. In dreams, displacement from the real object to the symbolic is unconscious; in literature, it is conscious. In psychopathology there is no abstraction in the use of the primary process; in literature, the abstract concept emerges through the primary process. In dreams, a person cannot distinguish between the world of the mind and the external world; in creation the artist knows that he creates a fiction. Arieti continually emphasizes the conscious, purposeful aspects of creativity. He postulates that creativity depends on a tertiary process which is "a special combination of primary and secondary process" (p. 12). Though the creative process consists primarily of primitive mental mechanisms, the primitive is not rejected but rather is integrated with normal, logical processes to create something new.

Roland (1978) also stresses integration. The artist's unconscious meanings are related to his more universal meanings. "His innermost experiences whether of psychosexual fantasy or some aspect of the self, are used in relationship to his more abstract and universal meanings. The artist's method of tapping his or her more unconscious or preconscious sources, is, I suspect, through the very images that are laden with more universal meanings and artistic purpose; i.e., poetic metaphors may contain the personal metaphorical as well" (p. 265). Notice that for Rothenberg, Arieti, and Roland, the universal meanings are autonomous, separate meanings which are integrated with the more unconscious, personal meanings. They are not, as they are for Holland, transformations of the personal. Universal meanings thus take on a legitimacy of their own.

We have seen a progressive movement in emphasis on the key factor in creativity—from unconscious conflict (Freud), to controlled regression to unconscious conflict (Kris), to defensive mechanisms and their relation to unconscious conflict (Holland), to the preconscious (Kubie), to the secondary processes (Rothenberg), and finally to the integration of all factors (Arieti, Roland). All these theorists use as their foundation the structural model of the mind. For them, the psyche can be seen in the functional aspects of the id, ego, and superego. These authors therefore focus on the intrapsychic elements in creativity. For Freud it was the id which dominated creativity; for Holland, the id and the ego defenses; for Rothenberg, the ego and its secondary processes.

Working from a different theoretical base, object relations theory, Winnicott (1971) sees creativity differently. For him, the creative process consists of both internal and active manipulation of the external. A child in playing uses external reality, a toy, in the service of personal reality. The playing occurs neither inside the mind of the child, nor outside the child, in an external reality which is not him and which he cannot control. Playing is not just fantasizing: "To control what is outside one has to *do* things, not simply to think or to wish, and *doing things takes time.* Playing is doing" (p. 41, Winnicott's italics). The creative process involves this interpenetration of the internal and the external. The artist's personal reality makes use of external reality, and he *does* something—he transforms it to something new. He fantasizes and controls an aspect of objective reality, and in doing so he creates a cultural product. The fantasies are externalized into the creative medium (for example, literature), and the creative product becomes his own individual product (Hamilton, 1975). But, at the same time, "an essential element of creativity is an *acceptance* of that which is outside the self" (Modell, 1970, p. 248). In art, the nonself is not just the artistic medium, but is also the tradition, past literature, for example. Creativity deals with the internal *and* with the external:

> The cultural transformation of the environment may be understood in part as a process modeled on the child's relation to his primary environment, that is, his mother. Separation anxiety (to which the fear of death is added) may also be the motive for the institution of a magically created environment. Both symbolic processes serve to mitigate the experience of total helplessness. (Modell, 1970, p. 248)

As we can see, theories of creativity follow the development of psychoanalytic theory: structural theory has been used as a basis, and now Winnicott provides a basis in object-relation theory. Where structural theory is more appropriate to oedipal conflicts, object relations is more concerned with the preoedipal. A theory of creativity based on the latter theory will stress the preoedipal processes of differentiating the internal from the external and of separating from the mother.

### THE AUTHOR'S PERSONALITY

In addition to being a manifestation of the creative process, literature relates to the personality of the author. The basic assumption underlying Freud's theory of creativity is that the literary work can reveal something about its author; he went from the content of the novel to the daydreams of the writer. Thereafter, this approach became popular. Analysts and literary critics psychoanalyze the author by focusing on his literary works as products of his psyche. In his study of *Hamlet* Ernest Jones presents the basic assumption clearly:

> It was a living person who imagined the figure of Hamlet with his behaviour, his reflections, and his emotions. The whole came from somewhere within Shakespeare's mind, and evidently from the inmost depths of that mind. Our search, therefore, must now continue in that direction. . . . We have to inquire into the relation of Hamlet's conflict to the inner workings of Shakespeare's mind. It is here maintained that this conflict is an echo of a similar one in Shakespeare himself. . . . (p. 115)

Using literary history (the sources of the play *Hamlet* and the use Shakespeare made of them), Shakespeare's other plays (thematic continuities after 1600), biographical speculation (regarding Shakespeare's relations with women at the time), and biographical information (the death of Shakespeare's father in 1601), Jones attempts to show that the oedipal concerns of Hamlet reflect the oedipal concerns of Shakespeare which were revitalized at the time of the writing.

*Après Jones, le deluge.* One of the most (in)famous psychoanalytic studies of an author is Marie Bonaparte's *The Life and Works of Edgar Allan Poe: A Psycho – Analytic Interpretation.* She connects Poe's fictive women and their "life in death" quality to Poe's mother who died when he was three. She links the murdered old men in Poe's tales to his stepfather John Allan. She attempts to relate the thematic elements of the stories to childhood fantasies that she surmises that Poe indulged in when young.

These kinds of studies have been the *bête noire* of psychoanalytic criticism. Once literary fantasies are related to personal fantasies, questions concerning the normality of the individual writer and creative writers in general arise. Freud himself vacillated on this question. At times, he implied that the artist neurotically turns away from reality, and at times he lauds the artist's insights. Followers of Freud have been more definitive in their conclusions. Bergler (1947) concludes that authors, frustrated by their mothers in the oral stage of development, obtain oral gratification from the manipulation of words, and stated that no writers he ever met could be considered normal. Stekel (1923) predated Bergler with a similar conclusion: "every artist is a neurotic" (p. 78).

But just as some critics have followed Freud's implication that artists are neurotic, others have followed his implication that they have a special talent. As early as 1938, W.R.D. Fairbairn concentrated on art's positive values which serve an ideal. Though creativity is seen as a way of restitution for destructive urges, the positive aspect of creation is more in focus here. Out of these destructive urges values and culture are created. Fenichel (1945) advises us that we should not use the concept of sublimation in an evaluative way. If creativity uses transformed sexual energy, it must be emphasized that it is *transformed* — it is not sexual, and that is the point. Sublimation of the instinctual impulses improves the function of the ego, and in part, artistic activity becomes progressive, not just regressive. Alexander (1948) makes roughly the same point when he notes that in creation, surplus energy is employed creatively and not selfishly, that is, for self-preservation or in the service of the self. Bychowski (1951), though believing creativity may serve defensive functions, considers that too much emphasis on this aspect and on other possibly neurotic aspects is illegitimate. Not only is the ego's reaction to unconscious impulses important, but the strength of the ego also goes into the art. In fact, the more art work is overdetermined, richer in form and content, the more developed the artist's personality. Both his unconscious impulses and the conscious ideals enter art. Finally, several authors already mentioned have stressed the adaptive and progressive functions of creativity — Kris (1952) speaks of the role of the ego's integrative powers, Kubie (1958) of the free mobility of the preconscious which allows the creation of the new, Rothenberg (1976) of cognitive processes under the control of the creator, and Roland (1978) of autonomous, universal meanings. All the preceding theorists are speaking of health, not neurosis.

CRITICISMS

Numerous criticisms have been levelled at the overall methodology itself and at particular psychoanalytic theories of creativity. Some critics have held that one should not try to relate the work of art to the artist at all. Most problematic is the sufficiency of data. In formulating hypotheses about the author's mind, the main source of material of the literary critic is the author's creative works. These are supplemented by biographical facts and, when available, nonfictive comments by the author, such as journals and letters. Slochower

(1971) calls this the "genetic pitfall" (p. 107). Once a hypothesis is made there is no test available for its validation (Griffin, 1951; Trilling, 1940). In clinical work, an interpretation is followed by a response from the patient. For instance, I interpreted to a patient, "You think I am going to punish you by returning your words like daggers if you express your anger." He responded, "Yeah," and added that he was surprised when his friends told him he was smug, and his words went out like daggers. His response showed that the interpretation led to a deepening of his insight. He now could begin to realize that *he* was hostile. With an author, there is no response; Shakespeare cannot reject, accept, or deepen Jones's interpretation of his oedipal concern.

Griffin (1951) takes this criticism a step further; he wonders how we know which character in a literary work represents the author. In other words, how does Jones know that the concerns of Hamlet, as opposed to those of Polonius, are Shakespeare's concerns? It seems that when we attempt to make statements about the author from his works, we are in murky territory. Some basic thoughts must be kept in mind. *Literature is a product of the human mind*; therefore, it must be related in some way to that mind. To hold that a poem is an artifact, not a person (Hahn, 1974) misses the point. To pretend it is not connected to a person is absurd. As Crews (1970) puts it:

> The recourse to "extra-literary" theory is not in itself, however, a methodological error. The simple fact that literature is made and enjoyed by human minds guarantees its accessibility to study in terms of broad principles of psychic and social functioning. (p. 1)

If one accepts the belief that the author's biography is relevant to the study of literature, one accepts the necessity for the application of psychoanalysis. Where there is biography, there is psychology, and where there is psychology, there is psychoanalysis, the only comprehensive theory of the human mind. Even if our hypotheses about the author are not absolutely verifiable, we can, in the final analysis, add significantly to his literature by understanding his relation to it (Trilling, 1940).

Another objection to focusing on the writer is that one may then ignore the formal aspects of the work. Fry (1924) holds that to center on fantasies and instincts leads us away from the distinct aesthetic elements of art. Wilson (1941) also complains that concentration on the writer's emotions ignores the formal. Slochower (1971) stresses this too but points to its solution as well. Through the use of ego psychology, one studies the adaptive functions of the ego. And as we have seen, the formal aspects of art are now being studied. Though stressing the defensive functions of form, Holland (1968) does examine images, word usage, and structure in poems meticulously. In contrast, Rothenberg (1978) objects that since the function of defensive mechanisms is to disguise, they cannot be responsible for aesthetic form. Just the same, he adds insight into the formal qualities of art. In arriving at his hypotheses concerning the cognitive processes involved in creativity, Rothenberg (1976) shows us how metaphors are constructed. In short, though the objection that the formal elements of art are ignored in psychoanalytic criticism may originally have been valid, new work is focusing on aspects of literature other than the content.

The most vociferous objection to the application of psychoanalysis to the author and his work has concerned the author's alleged neurosis. As we have seen, some early psychoanalysts stated quite bluntly that the artist is necessarily neurotic. Burke (1939) was one of the first critics to point out that while neurotic acts and poetic ones might both be symbolic, they were not necessarily totally similar. Trilling (1945), as well, objected to viewing art as neurotic and rightfully noted that nothing in the logic of psychoanalysis dictates such a view. Statements concerning the artist's neurosis are continually emphasized by critics when there are other available psychoanalytic data. For this reason, I have purposely reviewed numerous analysts who give attention to the "healthy" aspects of creation. At its base, this kind of objection seems founded on disapproval of the emphasis on unconscious factors in art. For instance, numerous early critics held that though there may be unconscious fantasy in a work of literature, the author had control over that fantasy (Trilling, 1940). Unfortunately, this criticism is still in vogue:

> Psychoanalysis shows in what way dreams and works of art are *substitutable*; their essential dissymmetry is yet to be understood. It is, in fact, one thing to fantasize at night in dreams. It is something else again to produce in a lasting object . . . for if the artist makes a lasting work, it is because he is successful in *structuring* his fantasies outside of himself. (Ricoeur, 1976, p. 23, Ricoeur's italics)

The point is well put, but though much more needs to be done to understand structuring, that work has begun, as we have seen in the work of Rothenberg, Arieti, Kubie, Kris, and Roland. In psychoanalytic theories of creation, there is beginning to be an integration of art's conscious, preconscious, and unconscious elements.

It has been held that if we regard an artist as neurotic, we somehow diminish art (Kazin, 1959). This is purely judgmental; the theory neither diminishes nor increases the stature of the artist or his art. It is no more than an added fact that may increase our understanding of the context of a work of art. The work may be affected by the author's neurosis, but this should not affect our evaluation of the art. In fact, it is possible for a literary work to be unaffected by its author's neurosis. In a study on the relation of psychopathology and creativity, Müller-Braunschweig (1975) concludes that " 'creative systems' may be formed and may function relatively unimpeded even in personalities with psychopathological traits" (p. 97).

There is one other important consideration in thinking about neurosis and the author. In Holland's comment on H.D., we see a confusion between defense and pathology and between symptom and character trait. Defensive functioning is not necessarily neurotic nor are character traits necessarily symptoms. (Technically, in psychoanalytic terminology, they are in fact of a different order. All human beings have defenses; all human beings have character traits. We could not *be* without them. We all have an unconscious, or rather, we all function unconsciously in certain ways. It is a mistake to think that pointing out a defense or an unconscious fantasy in an author or in a literary work is the same as ascribing a neurosis. Regarding Freud, Ricoeur (1976, p. 9) pointed out, "for him, there is no line of demarcation between the normal and the pathological." And recently an all-day meeting of the American Psychoanalytic Association failed to come to a consensus on what normality is.

## PSYCHOANALYSIS AND THE AUDIENCE

In his essay "Creative Writers and Day-Dreaming" (1908), Freud, in addition to looking at creativity, speculated on the reason for aesthetic pleasure. To Freud, the writer puts the readers into a situation where they can enjoy partly unacceptable daydreams without shame. Having disguised his own fantasies through the concealment of his *ars poetica*, the writer allows us to enjoy similar fantasies. In ending his essay on this note, Freud recognizes that he has just made a beginning: "This brings us to the threshold of new, interesting and complicated enquiries; but also, at least for the moment, to the end of our discussion" (p. 153). In fact, it is just in this new, interesting area where important and complex enquiries are now taking place.

The seed Freud planted was developed by Kris (1952) who treats art as a communication on the part of the artist and as the response of the audience. For Kris, art functions as an invitation to common mental experience: literature is a call to the reading audience to experience the literary product in common with collective humanity and with the artist. The artist, for example, may not be seeking admiration and recognition from the audience, as Freud held, but rather seeking alleviation of guilt over an unacceptable wish: "Response of others alleviates guilt" (p. 60). Kris attempts a more complex explanation of the interaction of the artist and the audience, however. In the work of art the artist's repressed impulses and wishes (id) communicate with his higher synthesizing functions (ego) — he becomes aware of his unconscious. There is a shift in psychic level on the part of the artist, from the primary processes of the id to the secondary processes of the ego. These processes are then submitted to the audience through the work of art. For Kris, the audience responds by a similar process. The reader of a literary work recreates the text. First, the reader relaxes control and allows an interplay with unconscious wishes; then he reasserts control and wards off the unacceptable wishes. As it is with the artist, the audience also experiences a shift in psychic level, and aesthetic communication becomes an experience of shared psychic levels. There is an interchange between the reader's and the writer's primary and secondary processes — their wishes, impulses, and fantasies, and their modes of controlling and elaborating them. Kris does not hold that this means the reader and writer are sharing the same content, that is, the same fantasy:

> What is made common to artist and audience is the aesthetic experience itself, not a preexistent content. . . . Communication lies not so much in the prior intent of the artist as in the consequent re-creation by the audience of his work of art. And re-creation is distinguished from sheer *reaction* to the work precisely by the fact that the person responding himself contributes to the stimuli for his response. (pp. 254–55)

One of the ways the reader contributes to the literary experience is through symbols. From the point of view of the artist, the literary symbol is overdetermined; it expresses many meanings and has multiple causes. From the point of view of the reader, it has multifaceted potential, that is, it can produce multiple effects. If the symbol evokes the reader's primary process, the reader contributes to the experience, expressed in his own interpretation or understanding of the literary text, of the meaning of the symbol. The contribution of Kris to our understanding of the relation of the audience to the art work involves: (1) the interaction of psychic processes between the art and audience; (2) the shift in psychic level of the audience; and (3) the active contribution of the audience to the aesthetic experience.

Holland (1968) elaborates these insights of Kris into a complete systematic theory of the reader's literary response to a work of literature. For Holland, the reader takes into himself the literary work with all its fantasies (unconscious content), with all its defenses, and with its management of those fantasies (formal aspects) and makes them his own:

> In effect, the literary work dreams a dream for us. It embodies and evokes in us a central fantasy; then it manages and controls that fantasy by devices that, were they in a mind, we would call defenses, but, being on a page, we call "form." And the having of the fantasy and feeling it managed give us pleasure. (p. 75)

The key to aesthetic pleasure is both the gratification of a forbidden fantasy *and* the control of that fantasy. Even the intellectual meaning we supply to a literary text in our interpretation of it acts as a defensive device to control the fantasy. Like Kris, Holland also holds that the reader himself contributes to the text by "constructing" the meaning. The reader supplies his own associations to the fantasy. In addition, he re-creates literary characters by endowing them with his own wishes and defenses. Holland believes that though the literary text provides a basis for the literary experience, the reader himself responds to that basis in his own personal way.

Though it is more developed, Holland's model is similar to that of Kris. Both stress: (1) the shift in psychic levels and meanings, (2) the interpenetration of the text and the reader's psyche, and (3) the re-creation of the text by the reader with his own personal associations.

In his more recent work, Holland (1973a, 1973b, 1975a, 1975b) has extended this last insight on the re-creation of the text. He no longer views the text as transforming a fantasy. The text transforms nothing, being merely the words on the page. The reader of the text does the transforming, and he does it according to his "identity theme," the central, unifying pattern which makes sense out of what he chooses and does.

> The overarching principle is: identity re-creates itself, or, to
> put it another way, style — in the sense of personal style —
> creates itself. That is, all of us, as we read, use the literary
> work to symbolize and finally to replicate ourselves. (p. 816)

According to Holland (1975b), the reader does this to the
work in three ways: (1) he finds what he characteristically
wishes or fears and must therefore re-create the usual ways he
deals with those wishes and fears; (2) he derives fantasies
expressing his own impulses which consequently give him
pleasure; and (3) he transforms the fantasy into an experience
of esthetic, moral, or intellectual significance.

As can be seen, for Holland, reading literature begins to
approach a totally subjective experience. Bleich (1975–76)
makes this view explicit:

> The discovery of a "true" meaning is less a matter of finding
> something objective that all must accept than finding some-
> thing subjective that others wish to accept. . . . Meaning is
> created as if the text did not exist, and the truth of our mean-
> ings is no less fictional than the text we read. (p. 40)

One psychoanalytic trend is toward seeing reading as subjective, and it is precisely on this interpretation that most critics
have pounced. As Crews (1975) puts it, "we don't go to criticism to discover Seymour's [one of Holland's student 'readers']
identity theme" (p. 554). For Crews, knowledge is a social
project. For him as well as others such as Waldoff (1975),
professional critics are the best contributors to that social project because their interpretations are more carefully reasoned.

Another objection is that this approach takes our concern
away from the text itself (Waldoff, 1975; Kaplan and Kloss,
1973) as if there are no limits on interpretations imposed by
what the text actually is. The author has put some feelings, as
well as language, in the text to which we respond. Drawing
originally on Bleich's work, Holland (1978) has recently attempted to meet these objections. Surveying the latest theories
on perception, cognition, and psycholinguistics, he shows
how perceiving and knowing are active processes involving
the person who is doing them.

> Reality, then, is never simply some fixed something "out
> there." . . . At no level in our continuum of cognition is there
> any way to separate a "subjective" from an "objective." . . .
> Everything we do replicates our individuality.

For Holland, the identity theme of each individual affects
what he perceives and knows in "reality." It first influences
the particulars focused on and then how one puts those particulars together. The application of this model to the reading of
literature does not work, however. For although in reality
there might be an infinity of particulars from which the perceiver discerns only his *personally selected* elements, there is
not an infinity of particulars in literature. The text is finite.
All readers work with the same text. Though they may work
with it in their own personal styles, it remains in some sense
the same, if only in the sense of having a limited number of
words. It does seem, then, that the text imposes at least some
limits. Here, Winnicott's concept of transitional space can
help. Art occurs in the "space" in which subjectivity and objectivity mingle. The subject brings his own fantasies to the
experience and so, in a sense, creates the experience. At the
same time, something external and real is involved, a reality
which allows itself to be created and molded (cf. Schwartz,
1973; Mollinger, S., 1978). As Winnicott always puts it, we
must be able to accept paradoxes.

# 2

# An Introduction
# to Psychoanalysis

It has frequently been pointed out that the word *psychoanalysis* has several meanings. First, it refers to a theory of the mind and mental processes, how they have developed, and why people do what they do. Second, it is an application of that theory to the treatment of patients. Finally, it is the use of that theory to explain occurrences usually studied by other fields of enquiry, such as sociology, anthropology, and art. My concern is primarily with the first and the third aspects of psychoanalysis, that is, with psychoanalysis as a theory of the mind that can serve as an explanatory model for literature. But before applying psychoanalysis, we first must understand the basic elements of the theory itself.

## METAPSYCHOLOGY

Constructing psychoanalytic theory from his observations and treatment of patients, Freud explored a patient's symptom until its meaning was revealed. From this exploration, he hypothesized more general principles according to which the mind operates. Recently, a line of thought has appeared in psychoanalytic theorizing which aims to differentiate more explicitly between those hypotheses relating to a particular patient, clinical theory, and those referring to the mind in general, metapsychological theory (Gill, 1976). Clinical theory deals with psychological meaning — what a particular act or symptom means to a particular person. These "meanings" can be generalized and can function as a background for the interpretation of similar acts or interactions. For example, A., a twenty-five year old woman, presents as her problem difficulty in breaking with her lover. As her description of her plight deepens, and as she associates further, it is seen that she feels that if she leaves him, he will go crazy, possibly kill himself. Furthermore, she feels she will be helpless without him. For A., separation means death for the other and helplessness for herself. Such an understanding becomes generalized when B., a twenty-year-old who comes to therapy because of a general lack of motivation, reveals that she too cannot separate from her lover to date another young man. She fears to "hurt" her present boyfriend and does not, even if it means limiting her acquaintances. In all likelihood, a dynamic similar to A.'s will be revealed. Possibly similar causes will be revealed as well. Clinical theory, or clinical hypotheses, include acts of interpretation which answer the question "why?" Why does a person perform such an act? (Wallerstein, 1974) It focuses on the subjective realm of experience. Why do A. and B. stick to their boyfriends? One answer is because of fear of their destructive impulses and of being left helpless themselves.

Though psychoanalysts' conceptions of what one does in a clinical situation and of the kinds of hypotheses made are clear, the meaning and function of "metapsychology" is not. Metapsychology has been referred to as : (1) a collection of assumptions on which psychoanalysis is based (Rapaport and Gill, 1959); (2) as a conceptual framework which provides a model for causal explanations and the formation of hypotheses (Lagache, 1955); (3) as a collection of propositions which rightfully belong in the natural sciences and not as a part of psychoanalysis (Gill, 1976); and (4) as propositions which answer "how" questions and thus make psychoanalysis a *general* psychological theory (Wallerstein, 1974).

According to the first definition of metapsychology, a psychoanalyst observes data in the consulting room, interprets connections between the data, and postulates clinical theories about the connections. He then theorizes about these, that is, he makes general assumptions which he believes will help order the data and the clinical theories. He deals not only with what is observed in the person's behavior but with what is going on in the person's mind. For instance, a person might value discipline. The effect of this value on the person's behavior might be explored, and theories about it constructed. Psychoanalysis goes further; it theorizes that the mind can be seen in terms of its functioning. Similar functions, like valuation with its particular values such as discipline, can be grouped together in what is called a structure. According to the first definition, the assumption that the human mind can be seen in terms of structures which perform particular functions is a metapsychological theory.

The second definition is a more limited one. Here metapsychological statements are those which provide a model for causal explanations. When one says that a person works eighteen hours a day because he values self-discipline, one is referring to the psychic structure which performs an evaluative function and affects behavior. Since the statement refers to causation, it is metapsychological.

According to the third definition, statements about the physical substrate of psychological functioning should be relegated to metapsychology and kept apart from psychological concepts. One might say that a person is rigidly self-disciplinarian because he was born with a strong aggressive drive which he turns upon himself. That part of the statement which deals with the aggressive drive is a biological statement. Though many analysts believe that our understanding of these drives should be integrated into our knowledge of normal emotional development and behavior, others believe that only biologists should concern themselves with such drives.

The fourth definition subsumes the others. By answering "how" questions, psychoanalysis becomes a general psychology. (1) How is it that a person continually disciplines himself and others? An answer is that the mind is made up of relatively stable and nonchanging structures, one of which concerns itself with values such as discipline. (2) How does it come about that a person works eighteen hours a day? A mental structure which values severe discipline influences his behavior. (3) How does discipline become so severe? An innate aggressive drive might be extremely powerful. As we have just seen, all three perspectives may go into explaining "how" an action occurs.

Since theory is necessary for further insight (in the consulting room, there is a constant interaction between theoretical constructs in the analyst's mind and the contributions of the patient), this last view is probably the most useful. Theory needs to be stated, structured, formalized, and made explicit, because whenever we think psychologically we are implicitly drawing on theories, especially those with common-sense assumptions. When we speak of people, our talk embodies inferential psychological knowledge. To avoid theory is to avoid an ever-present reality; to confront and develop it will lead, in the end, to clarity regarding our basic assumptions. In addition, avoidance of theory ignores an essential aspect of observation and of the psychoanalytic process:

> The everyday tools of all analysts, whatever their insight into or evaluation of theory, include of necessity not only "descriptive" but also "explanatory" concepts. Every psychoanalytic case report, however "factual," is replete with inference based upon theoretical assumptions. (Hartmann, Kris, and Loewenstein, 1953, p. 119)

Theory is a necessity, even though it may seem abstract at times, apparently irrelevant at times, obscure at times, and even mechanical at times. Most important, however, is the need to remain clear on the kind of question being confronted and answered in a psychoanalytic statement — a why or how question — and what kind of proposition is being made, a psychological one or a metapsychological one.

To illustrate some basic psychoanalytic, metapsychological points, the example of a particular patient with specific symptoms would be helpful. C., a thirty-five-year-old single office worker who wanted to be an actress, came to treatment suffering from compulsive symptoms. During the course of her treatment, she revealed a fantasy which helped her achieve sexual climax. In it, she was usually nude and was beaten on the rear by a man and a woman.

Based on a metapsychological hypothesis that all mental phenomena, from the significant to the trivial, are determined rather than random, psychoanalytic theory would first propose that this fantasy has a cause. According to another metapsychological hypothesis, this cause may not be immediately apparent. Psychic phenomena can be unconscious as well as conscious, that is, phenomena may be located in different areas of the mind, metaphorically speaking. (This view is known technically as the topographical model of the mind.) On the one hand, is a conscious wish that can be delayed and thought upon; it can be dealt with by the secondary processes, perception, cognition, and memory. When one is hungry in the afternoon, one can perceive an apple on the table, know that it rather than a shoe will satisfy the hunger wish. One may eat it immediately or wait for the expected full course meal which one remembers will come at six o'clock in the evening.

On the other hand, unconscious material, especially a wish, operates according to the primary process, a type of thinking in which there is the lack of a sense of time, of negatives, and of conditionals, and the use of allusion and symbolic representation. The unconscious wish seeks immediate gratification. Since one is not aware of an unconscious desire, a substitute gratification may be achieved.

C.'s fantasy plays a larger role in her sexual climax than

actual, physical stimulation. It is a gratifying substitution. Though conscious, the fantasy is symbolic for something else. Over a period of time, the meaning of the fantasy (an aspect of clinical theory) began to emerge. She felt the man in the fantasy was authoritative, independent, glamorous, kind, and protective. He was a man who "could tell the world where to get off." The woman was big, a heavy, maternal figure, a black or Italian "mama." She finally said, "Perhaps they are my parents." Being beaten is both a hostile act and an erotic one, for she is nude. Here we see that unconsciously one thing can represent another, substitute for it, and, in fact, can be contradictory. Asked why she is being beaten, she replied, "For sexual and hostile thoughts." When she was a child she worried about being beaten for masturbating. Now she is furious at her mother for inhibiting her sexually by making her think sex is dirty. Although it is a punishment which expiates guilt, the beating is sexual also — it brings about a climax.

Explaining how these distortions and contradictions come about, psychoanalysis constructs a metapsychological hypothesis (the dynamic model). Mental phenomena are the result of the interaction of forces. In the fantasy, one force is the wish for sexual gratification; another force is the hostile impulse. There is the guilt over sexual impulses and also the guilt over C.'s hostility toward her mother. It is the interaction of these forces which produces the fantasy — its symbols, its distortions, and its hidden logical illogic. Unable to tolerate the explicit presence of her parents in the fantasy, she disguises them by imagining any man or woman. Unable to tolerate overt sexuality in the fantasy, she is nude in order to be beaten, not to be made love to. The fantasy draws her attention to the beating and away from the sexuality. It is with these conflicts within the mind that psychoanalysis is particularly concerned.

In a further attempt to explain the source of this fantasy and how it comes about, psychoanalysis proposes that there is psychic energy which can be transformed, distributed, and expended. C. has a sexual impulse; it must be directly gratified, indirectly gratified as in the fantasy, or controlled totally. Wherever directed, the energy must be expended (the economic model). Whichever path is taken, energy is at work, the energy of the impulse and the energy which attempts to control it, and the source of this energy is instinctual. This energy theory is undergoing more and more criticism. Many analysts (for example, Schafer, 1976) think it is more profitable to eliminate this metapsychological hypothesis from psychoanalysis. Though the concept of energy may need to be revised and revitalized, perhaps, psychoanalysis does seem to require some basic concept of intensity (Mayman, 1976) whether it comes from biological instincts or from instinctual drive patterns.

More importantly, psychoanalysis questions how such a fantasy comes about. What is its origin? How has it developed (the genetic model)? It postulates that the past affects the present and that past traumatic events produce present mental phenomena. Past fantasies about, and interactions with, significant figures, such as parents, result in present personality. C.'s parents' attitudes toward sexual activity brought about C.'s guilty attitude and thus, in part, produced the self-punishment in the fantasy. Even more specific is the guilt resulting from sexual desires toward the particular man represented in the fantasy. C. said that he was authoritative and protective, perhaps her parent, that is, her father. In fact, C. frequently has desires for married men, like her father was and is. She once negatively hinted at her problem: "nothing specific ever happened to me like a father being seductive, calling his daughter a slut, or beating his child." Freud (1919) put it clearly: "*The beating-phantasy has its origins in an incestuous attachment to the father*" (p. 198, Freud's italics). C.'s childhood fantasies about her father, unresolved in her youth, now appear in her contemporary fantasy: she has sexual contact with him in the beating.

To further explain particular mental phenomena, psychoanalysis postulates a model for the mind in terms of structure based on functions (the structural model). As Harrison (1970)

puts it, "established functions tend to 'structuralize' in the
sense of forming steady states that resist change and do not
have to be created anew repeatedly. Thus, the so-called structures are really systematic groupings of functions forming
theoretical constructs. In a sense, they are logical artifacts
that are inferred from behavior" (p. 131). Psychoanalysis
groups together (in what is called the id) instinctual impulses
and the images and fantasies associated with them, like C.'s
sexual desire for her father and hostile impulse toward her
mother. These are at times unconscious because another part
of the mind (the superego) finds them unacceptable, that part
which includes the values and attitudes internalized from the
external world. C. has internalized her parents' attitude that
sex is bad, even though she intellectually feels otherwise;
herein lies a source of conflict. Other mental functions (ego)
attempt to satisfy both the instincts seeking gratification and
the attitudes which oppose them. Perception, memory, and
cognition are used to find satisfaction. When the impulses
need to be controlled because they are unacceptable, defense
mechanisms are used. In the fantasy, the sexual desire is made
unconscious, and C.'s interest is displaced from her father to a
less clearly delineated man.

Finally, there is one other perspective that can be considered. How has C.'s relation to her environment affected her
fantasy (the adaptive point of view)? How has she used this
fantasy to adapt to reality? In her family, both hostile and
sexual impulses were viewed as negative; her mother would
ignore C.'s anger and would downgrade sex. To keep the
approval of her mother, C. thought that she had to incorporate the mother's views as her own. When young, C. saw this
as her only option in adapting to the environmental forces
around her.

## DEVELOPMENT OF THE PERSONALITY

Metapsychological hypotheses allow the analyst to order
the data he observes; as Hans Loewald puts it, metapsychology is concerned with ways of observing, ordering, and con-

ceptualizing analytic material (Meissner, 1976). It also allows us to order both clinical material, which Freud pioneered in collecting, and data from direct observation of infants, which later analysts like René Spitz (1965) have focused on, into stages of normal development of the personality. Using the structural model, which groups together similar functions, we can focus on which instinctual (id) impulses (with their attached fantasies) are of primary importance at a particular time, which ego functions (those which organize experience and attempt to master reality), structures, and identifications are formed, which anxieties are experienced in certain periods, and which superego identifications (parental values and prohibitions which the person makes his own) are made and when. Using the adaptive model, we can delineate what kinds of interactions take place between the child and the environment (also called object relations). We can see how the child views the other person, especially the parents, and how he regards his own self and how the other takes on an identity for him. Using the dynamic model, we can see what kinds of internal forces are at work and what kinds of conflicts take place. According to the genetic assumption, these conflicts lead to problems later in life.

THE FIRST MONTH OF LIFE

During the first month of life, the infant is just beginning to express varied functions which can conceptually be grouped into mental structures. The infant's main need is food, and his main experience is hunger. In terms of the id, we can say that his instinctual impulses center on his mouth and oral cavity. In fact, the neonate's one directed behavior is an innate "sucking reflex" (Spitz, 1957). Though psychoanalysis usually distinguishes between two kinds of instinctual impulses, sexual and aggressive, at this stage in development, it is difficult to see them separately (Hartmann, Kris, and Loewenstein, 1949). In the neonate's sucking, we can see erotic (sensual) gratification and aggressive (assertive) gratification. Any aggressivity is expressed through the neonate's activity: crawling movements, lifting the head, rolling, clenching hands, and making fists. The neonate is not passive; he both seeks and avoids (Weil, 1976). The infant's internal feeling state is quiescent (homeostatic) when his needs are satisfied and displeasurably tense when they are not. He functions according to the pleasure principle. If he is not actively retaining pleasurable feelings, he is certainly wishing to eliminate unpleasurable ones. For example, he will try to avoid having his nose wiped.

Though ego functions, such as perception and cognition, are present from the beginning in the sense that they have the capacity to mature, the ego needs to be developed as an organized structure through exchanges between the organism and its internal and external environment (Spitz, 1966; Axelrad and Brody, 1970). For example, the neonate's functions become more focused from apprehending internal tensions, discomfort, satiation and external intrusions, such as being touched, held, comforted, picked up, and put down.

In the infant, the ego forms in conjunction with the emergence of the feeling of anxiety (Axelrad and Brody, 1970):

> Anxiety is one of the principal affects with which the ego is ushered into being; as the infant organism perceives some dystonic condition in his own body and perceives as well his own immediate, involuntary response to the condition, the ego is born and exercises a primary function. (p. 9)

The neonate begins to exercise some control over himself, at least in the sense that he can organize his experience. During the first month of life, the neonate does not experience real anxiety, but he does have the capacity to respond to sensations and to begin to organize them into perceptions (Axelrad and Brody, 1970).

From the point of view of adaptation and object relations, that is, the interaction of the neonate with the environment, the ego begins to be built from the mental images the infant forms and the memories (memory traces) the infant can retain. These come from his interactions with objects, the people toward whom the neonate directs his instincts and wishes for gratification. While there are actual external objects, there are also the internal objects, the imagined representation in the mind of the external object. At this early stage the neonate has no conception of the actual, external other person; he is in his own autistic world. Even when food is introduced into the infant's mouth, he continues to cry; he is aware only of his own sensations and not that the food has arrived and that gratification is near (Spitz, 1966). It is as if there is a wall separating him from external reality. But it is a protective one, a stimulus barrier, which screens out possibly overwhelming stimuli which he could not handle. His mother also acts to protect him from intrusive stimuli, loud noises, biting dogs, and clawing cats. Though the neonate is cut off from the other person, his identity is influenced by the other. Through imprinting, an innate disposition to learn the parent (Gray, 1958), the neonate within six weeks imprints the mother as someone of the same species (Axelrad and Brody, 1970). The neonate identifies as a human being, not as a dog or cat. This also sets the stage for becoming like the mother in certain ways.

In summary, for about a month, (1) the neonate's instinctual impulses are not differentiated and are primarily oral; (2) his ego is beginning to form via the interaction with environment and the consequent anxiety; and, (3) since the neonate has no conception of the other person, his relation to the external other is confined to the innate process of imprinting.

THE FIRST YEAR

As the infant begins to mature after the first month of life, the mental structures begin to form and be organized. Though his impulses remain focused on the oral cavity, they are more structured — he takes in, spits out, sucks and bites. As Erikson (1950) says, "he lives through, and loves with, his mouth. . ." (p. 72).

The ego continues to develop through its interaction with the environment. Satisfactory experiences are introjected, reproduced by images in the mind. The mental representations of these experiences include an image of the self in the experience, an image of the object in the experience, and the affect, here positive, of the experience (Kernberg, 1976). If the infant is well fed, he forms a memory of that good feeding, an image in his mind of what the feeding was like. There are three parts to this mental image. First, he remembers himself as pleased and gratified, so he has an image of a satisfied self. Second, he remembers the other person as gratifying and pleasing him and consequently has an image of a satisfying other. Third, he remembers the whole experience as satisfying; associated with the images of himself and of the other person is the feeling of pleasure.

Negative experiences are also introjected; if the infant is hungry, an image of a frustrating object and an image of a frustrated self are formed under the influence of the affect of displeasure which accompanies the hunger. All images of positive experiences are grouped together; so too are all negative ones. There are two separate groups of images, one pleasurable and one unpleasurable. The negative ones are eliminated as being unpleasurable; the infant does not want memories of bad experiences. At this early stage, the negative images are ejected through the defense mechanism of projection; they are not considered part of the self, "not me" (Jacobson, 1964). The state of the ego becomes all pleasurable and contains all good images.

At this point, the infant has begun to move out of his autistic world and attach himself to the mother in a symbiotic unity (Mahler, 1968). This attachment depends on the sufficiency of the interaction with the mother:

> The greater the failure of the mother to provide those good-enough experiences in which she attunes herself to and responds to the child's state of being, the less likely it is that affective attachment will develop. (Horner, 1975, p. 99)

The infant still has no conception of the outer world, and the mother is still not recognized as separate from him. He cannot really distinguish between who he is and who his mother is, where he ends and his mother begins. The infant feels rather that he is one with the fulfiller of his needs; they are a unity. To be precise, he really can not have separate mental images of himself and the other person; the images consist of fused self-object images. Experiencing pleasure or gratification of his needs, the infant feels that the unified infant-mother image is good, and an internal sense of goodness grows. It is not that "I am good and mother is good" but instead, "I combined with the other am good." The same is true of negative images; experiencing pain or frustration of his needs, the infant feels the unified infant-mother image is bad. An internal sense of badness develops, which as we have said, is projected out of the self.

At this stage, internal images become suffused with a quality of omnipotence. Feeling a need, wishing for its satisfaction, and then actually experiencing that satisfaction, the infant thinks that he is in control and powerful enough to satisfy himself by just wishing. When the infant feels hunger, immediately food arrives and satiates him. This is experienced as an omnipotent satisfaction of his own needs. But just as he can omnipotently create his own fulfillment, he can omnipotently destroy. When frustrated, the infant becomes totally enraged and destructive. If the infant feels hunger, and if food does not arrive, frustration and rage take over. This is experienced as an all-powerful destruction, because for the infant the affect is intense and overwhelming. It radiates over all the elements of the infant's perception during the particular experience (Kernberg, 1976). Both kinds of internal self images — good (satisfied) and bad (frustrated and enraged) — as well as those of the object, become suffused with this omnipotent affect.

It is essential for the infant to have his sense of omnipotence supported by the mother. At the same time that the infant hallucinates his satisfaction, the good mother actually provides that satisfaction. When she does, external reality matches the hallucination, and through experiences of this type the infant develops a sense of who he is, a sense of himself.

> The good-enough mother meets the omnipotence of the infant and to some extent makes sense of it. She does this repeatedly. A True Self begins to have life, through the strength given to the infant's weak ego by the mother's implementation of the infant's omnipotent expressions. (Winnicott, 1960, p. 145)

From these experiences the infant also develops a sense of trust in the external world (Erikson, 1968). The infant realizes that desire and reality are not inevitably opposed (Rycroft, 1968). While an actual satisfying mother increases the infant's sense of omnipotent goodness and trust, a frustrating one increases his sense of omnipotent badness. Since this badness is projected, the infant then distrusts and hates the world.

While symbiotic fusion with mother is at its height, the infant has imprinted the mother as his own mother and has become attached to her as the specific gratifier of his needs (Axelrad and Brody, 1970; Bowlby, 1969). In imprinting his mother, the infant develops another aspect of his identity: "The very extremeness of the symbiotic relation of the human child to his mother — usually described as the long dependency of the human infant on the mother — becomes the very source of the emergence of *human* identity. . . . The infant is one with the mother, but simultaneously there is a primary relatedness of a part to a whole" (Lichtenstein, 1961, p. 202). Being a part, the infant begins to express an identity in terms of what he is for someone else, his mother. How she holds, touches, responds to, and stimulates the infant reflects her unconscious wishes regarding him. The infant is "transformed into an organ or an instrument for the satisfaction of the mother's unconscious needs" (Lichtenstein, 1961, p. 207). For instance, instead of holding the infant when he needs to be held, the mother may hold him when she needs to. From this experience, the infant later may become one who exists to gratify the other person, even at the expense of his own needs. This way of relating becomes a part of who he is.

Most researchers hold that from three months old the infant, having begun to distinguish between inner and outer stimuli, can temporarily delay his own need. He can begin to operate on the reality principle, that is, he begins to take into account the conditions imposed on him by the external world. At six to eight months, in terms of mental structures the ego, whose function it is to master reality and find gratification, begins to be organized. This is signalled by the infant's distinction between his own mother and other people; he smiles at her but may experience anxiety when others appear. Anxiety is experienced over the possibility that needs may not be fulfilled, which would result in annihilation. The ego, then, must tolerate the delay in gratification and find means to obtain it. It does so by using the maturing ego functions, cognition, memory, and perception. If upon perceiving a stranger, the infant can remember that his mother has returned previously and thus can think that she will return again soon, the anxiety may be contained.

Some frustration of needs also leads to the beginning differentiation of the internal mental images of the self and the object (external reality). As Winnicott (1963) puts it, "the frustrating aspect of object behavior has value in educating the infant in respect of the existence of a not-me world" (p. 181). More importantly, gratification leads to the differentiation. The image of the good self-object differentiates into an image of an internal good self and an image of an internal good object between the third and ninth months (Kernberg, 1975). The infant begins to see the outer world, not as totally separate from himself, but as a satisfier or frustrator of his needs. When the mother is satisfying, the infant sees her as totally good; when she is frustrating, he sees her, in fusion with himself, as totally bad. Within his mind the infant constructs from a satisfying mother, an image of a good mother and in turn an image of a good self who is worthy of being satisfied. From a frustrating mother, the infant forms an image of a bad-self object. When satisfactorily fed, the infant feels good and retains an image of a good self, a self which feels good, and an image of a good mother, a mother who makes the infant feel good. When unsatisfactorily fed, the infant retains an image of frustration. A bad self which cannot satisfy itself and a bad other who is unsatisfying are confused as one.

As the infant begins to differentiate the good self from the good other, he experiences anxiety over the loss of the object which gives him nurturance and pleasure. On the one hand, this can encourage the development of ego functions which would allow him to more actively obtain pleasure on his own. Since the infant realizes that the other is different from him, the infant then realizes he must make do on his own. On the other hand, defenses are also provoked. The infant is basically helpless in satisfying his own needs. When he experiences frustration, he loses his awareness of the autonomous other and projects the bad self-object and the negative affect which goes with it. At the same time, in order to feel safe, he merges his internal image of himself with the internal image of the good mother. The infant uses his sense of omnipotence, that of being a part of an all-powerful, need-fulfilling unity, to defend against his own sense of helplessness. As Modell (1968) puts it, "*the capacity for magical thought mitigates the danger of catastrophic anxiety through the creation of illusion of lack of separateness between the self and the object*" (Modell's italics, p. 23). The infant feels that if he is one with his powerful mother he will not be frustrated. He pretends as if a frustrating mother could not exist.

By splitting off the bad self-object, the infant also protects the inner good mother from his rage at being frustrated. If the bad, frustrating mother does not exist, the infant need not feel angry, and then the good, satisfying mother is safe. The rage, which increases the image of the bad self-object, is also projected out and thereby makes the environment seem malevolent. Eliminating his own raging self-image, the world becomes threatening. A further development can take place here: since the infant and the good mother are now endangered by the threatening world, the infant, in order to handle this problem, takes the bad back into his mind. He turns the bad against himself in order to preserve the other person as a good object in a masochistic maneuver for survival. Instead of being angry at mother, the infant is angry at himself. The internalized image of the bad self-object can be considered a forerunner of the superego (Kernberg, 1976).

Another way of denying separateness is to make use of a transitional object. The object is a real, external object, like a teddy bear or doll, which, in the infant's mind, magically protects him from danger and is there to serve his loving and hating needs. In his relationship to the object, the infant can have his illusions fulfilled by reality, and, in a sense, he can repudiate the not-me external world (Winnicott, 1971), for the object is both real *and* what the infant makes of it.

At this point, major developments have occurred. From a structural point of view, the id impulses have been mainly oral with aggressive drives being expressed in activity as well. The ego (1) has developed its functions, such as perception, memory, motility; (2) has begun to experience anxiety over annihilation and the loss of the gratifying object; (3) has formed defensive modes, such as introjection (the taking in of images), projection, idealization, turning against the self, and splitting (the keeping apart of good and bad images); and (4) has built up internal images — first of a fused good self-object and a fused bad-self object, and secondly of a separate good object and good self. The superego has not yet been organized.

From the adaptive point of view, we have seen how the internal psychic structures have developed in conjunction with the changes in object relations. At first, the ego shields itself from stimuli with the help of the mother. Then, as the infant attaches symbiotically to the mother, he begins to learn about reality and how to delay his needs as well as obtain satisfaction from the omnipotent (m)other with whom he feels merged in a dual unity. Slowly he begins to distinguish his mother as his mother and himself as distinct from her. At the same time, he develops a sense of who he is in terms of his relationship with her (Mahler et al., 1975).

From the dynamic point of view, internal conflicts are not between the ego, id, and superego, but rather between the self and object images, between the infant's own wishes and an internalized image of mother's wishes or prohibitions (Dorpat, 1976). The infant attempts to protect his mental image of his good self and his mental image of his good mother, mostly by eliminating images of frustration. It must be understood that these are intrapsychic dynamics which concern the mental images the infant has of the mother; these images do not necessarily represent the actual behavior of the real, living mother.

THE SECOND YEAR

Entering his second year, the child develops his mental structures further. His instinctual impulses are organized around the anus as toilet training begins. The child experiences retention of the feces as the keeping of a loved object and elimination as the destruction of it. Here lies the basis for numerous attitudes. Ambivalence is seen in the child's reaction to his own feces as a representation of an object apart from him. Keeping it, he loves it. Flushing it down the toilet, he hates or destroys it. The feces is the child's first possession, and his keeping it in and to himself or his giving it up to his mother provide models for later attitudes toward possessions, such as money. Being toilet trained, the child is both controlled by his mother and encouraged to control himself; important attitudes to control of self and of other also begin here.

His ego has now organized his locomotor apparatus, and he can now move much more freely. As we shall see, this mobility has a great effect on his relations with other people. Early aspects of his superego will be formed from the internalizations of his interactions with them and their values, such as control and discipline.

From an object relations perspective, the maturation of his autonomous functions, like cognition, allow him further internal discriminations. Having already differentiated the good self image and the good object image, the child can now distinguish between the bad self and bad object images. This is accompanied by an increasing recognition of the separate existence of the other and therefore of himself. Because the child has not yet integrated the varied images of himself and the other, now more clearly distinguished as the mother, he vacillates between seeing himself as all good or all bad and between seeing his mother as all good or all bad. He does not recognize that he can have both good and bad qualities simultaneously, nor that his mother can be both a gratifier and frustrator. His own identity and the identities of others are still diffuse at this point.

Since through maturation the child can move physically away from his mother, he begins to separate from her (Mahler et al., 1975). Separating from the mother can be seen as dangerous, as being abandoned without the means of surviving on one's own. A child will move away from his mother to play, but he will keep an eye on her and at times run back to her to make sure she is still there for him. Since the child in reality still needs his mother, in his mind he will split off or disassociate the image of the "bad mother" in order to protect his internal relationship with the image of the "good mother" (Kernberg, 1976). Inasmuch as the child through maturation is being pushed toward being an individual while at the same time he still has not totally differentiated his identity from that of his mother, another anxiety may arise. To be reunited with the internal image of the good mother means to be reengulfed and lose one's self. In terms of behavior, the child, to preserve who he is, may become negative and defiant, for example, always saying no. The child moves toward being an individual with the fear of being helpless on his own. He moves back to mother with the fear of being engulfed and losing his precarious identity.

The interaction of the mother and child over the child's anal impulses occurs within this framework of good and bad internal images. As the child grows he becomes more sober as he realizes that he is not omnipotent; he now needs the approval of his mother. A new anxiety appears: he is now con-

cerned with the loss of the mother's love as his mother begins
to put limits on his actions. His ego uses specific defense mechanisms. To please her he will submit and perhaps use reaction
formation, replacing his anal impulses to be messy with clean-
liness. He will be tempted to exercise his own initiative and
control, but may submit to the control of the other person; he
may do something his mother's way, rather than his own. To
please her, he will displace his anger at her for controlling him
onto others or will turn it against himself. In terms of internal
mental images, the child needs to feel approved and loved by
the internal image of the good object; to relieve the anxiety of
losing the internal mother's love, he will constantly try to ally
himself with goodness, to do the right thing, and to perfect
himself. As Lidz (1968) puts it, "the child is apt to consider the
mother who gives and bestows love as the 'good mother' and
the frustrating mother as another person — the 'bad mother.'
Similarly, he is apt to consider himself as two children: a good
pleasing child and a naughty, contrary one. The 'good child'
may wish to renounce responsibility for the 'bad child' " (p.
172). The mother, who in the child's eyes, demands perfection
can become a harsh image in the child's superego.

### THE THIRD YEAR AND AFTER

Near the end of the third year the infant's object relations
change. He begins to see others as complete human beings
with needs and desires of their own. They do not just exist to
satisfy him. Internally, within his ego, his images of the good
mother and the bad mother begin to coalesce, and he constructs a picture of his mother as being both good and bad at
the same time. He can continue his relationship to her even if
he is frustrated; she no longer exists just to satisfy his needs. His
images of himself are unified, and his identity becomes solidified. Viewing others as whole people, he can now experience
guilt and concern. In addition to the unified self and object
images, the child creates an image of an ideal self and an ideal
object which reflect in fantasy the now lost all-good images of

the past (Kernberg, 1976) when an all-good mother existed just for him and satisfied all his needs.

His recognition of himself as a person and others as persons coincides with a new instinctual stage, his genital impulses which are now coming to the fore. The child becomes curious about the differences in the sexes, childbirth, and his parents' sexuality. The child may hypothesize that impregnation occurs orally, or that it is related to urination. Birth may be believed to occur through the anus or navel. He may imagine that intercourse depends on the domination of the father over the mother and that she is being injured during it.

New anxieties and new ways of handling them by the ego appear. When the young boy notices the absence of the penis on a woman he may at first deny this fact. Freud's "Little Hans" (1909) thought his mother, who appeared so large to him, would have a penis as big as that of a horse. Then he may try to explain the fact; he feels that perhaps the penis has been cut off girls by their parents as the mother of Little Hans threatened to send for the doctor to cut off his penis.

As the genital impulses of the boy increase, they become attached to the mother, for, after all, she desires the father who has a penis. Though the boy wishes to be like his father, he recognizes that his father stands in the way of his attaining his mother and desires to eliminate the father as a competitor appear. Freud said to Hans, "You thought then that if only Daddy were to die, you'd be Daddy," and Hans answered, "Yes." This hostile impulse toward the father produces in the boy a fear of retaliation, perhaps in the form of castration. To handle this dilemma, the boy, using a new defensive mode, represses his erotic desire for the mother and internalizes the fearful authority of the father, which becomes a value and threat in the superego.

The young girl develops slightly different anxieties. When she notices that she does not have a penis, her self-esteem is wounded, and she may want one. Recent psychoanalytic thinking emphasizes that the girl becomes interested in the penis, not because she wants to be a boy, but rather in order to detach herself from her mother and become autonomous as a woman (Torok, 1970; Chasseguet-Smirgel, 1970). Slowly, giving up her desire for a penis and, as a replacement, wanting a baby, she turns toward her father as a love object. The father is idealized to make up for the disappointments that the little girl feels she has experienced in her relationship with her mother (Chasseguet-Smirgel, 1970). Knowing that her mother is a competitor for him, however, she now fears her mother who might become angry and might abandon her.

At this stage, the mental structure of the child is more formalized. In fact, it must be cohesive even to experience these genital impulses:

> The presence of a firm self is a precondition for the experience of the Oedipus complex. Unless the child sees himself as a delimited, abiding, independent center of initiative, he is unable to experience the object-instinctual desires that lead to the conflicts and secondary adaptations of the oedipal period. (Kohut, 1977, p. 227)

Now being able to repress these unacceptable impulses, the ego is confronted by the id that organizes these impulses. On the other side, the ego is confronted by a consolidated superego which is now composed of the prohibitions and demands of the parents during this oedipal phase (for example, the prohibition of the parent of the opposite sex as a sex object), as well as the ideal images of the self and object (ego ideal) and the much earlier image of the bad self-object (Kernberg, 1976). The dynamic model of the mind now is useful for understanding the psyche. Whereas earlier conflicts were between the internal images of the self and other, now the ego must mediate, usually through compromise, between the instinctual impulses (like incest fantasies) and the superego demands (like incest taboos).

With this consolidation of the mental structure, the child now has the energy to focus on other tasks. Though it was first thought that sexual drives became latent between the ages of six and twelve, it is now acknowledged that they continue.

What has changed, however, is the capability of the ego. The ego, with the superego, now has better control over the instincts. Since such ego functions as perception, memory, learning, and thinking, have become consolidated (Blos, 1962), the child can begin to accomplish other tasks in society and in school. His object relations begin to expand. He becomes aware of his peers and his teachers, as well as his family, and he must learn to relate to them. Likewise, he must learn to adapt to school work and chores — to become industrious (Erikson, 1968) and responsible (Lidz, 1968).

With the onset of puberty, instinctual impulses again become important, and they revive the early stages of development — symbiotic, separation-individuation, and oedipal. The boy must first cope with envy of the female's capability to have a baby and his fear of castration by the powerful mother; he does this by turning away from girls (Blos, 1962). The young girl must cope with the pull toward the overwhelming mother; she does so by turning toward heterosexuality. In later adolescence, both boy and girl must cope with the revived oedipal complex with its sexuality and aggression toward the parents. They do this by seeking heterosexual objects outside the family. At the same time, the youth must deal with his separation from his parents and the necessity for going out on his own. This revives the earlier separation-individuation stage. Part of being able to leave the family depends on the attainment of an identity: a sexual, an ideological, and an occupational identity (Erikson, 1968). Though there are other developmental and psychological tasks to be faced later, when the youth has confronted and mastered these tasks in adolescence, his basic character is established.

This rough sketch of psychoanalytic theory of the child's earliest years gives some idea of the kinds of human experience psychoanalysis is concerned with and the kinds of statements it makes.

## SOME OBJECTIONS TO PSYCHOANALYSIS

Ever since its beginnings in the early 1900s psychoanalysis

has been controversial. This controversy has been based, at least in part, on misunderstandings and misperceptions of what psychoanalysis is and what the psychoanalytic process entails. Freud himself complained of "badly informed opponents." Today analysts are somewhat pejoratively known as "shrinks." Of course, there are numerous criticisms of psychoanalysis, some valid and some not so valid. Some criticism is from a scientific perspective and some is from the perspective of the general populace. I want particularly to consider those scientific objections and later those current perceptions or misperceptions popularly held today.

In the intellectual community, a frequent objection to psychoanalysis concerns its scientific status. These criticisms are: (1) that its theoretical formulations cannot be verified; (2) that its data is private (gathered in the consulting room), and therefore the data cannot be countered with alternative evidence; (3) that it uses unscientific support from other areas, such as mythology; (4) that its interpretations and data can be tainted by suggestion on the part of the analyst; and (5) that its formulations are too metaphoric (Burnham, 1967). The first criticism, that psychoanalytic theory cannot be verified, is incorrect. Although verification may be difficult, it is being done. In fact, the theory as a whole has not been disproved, and parts have been supported. As Kline (1972) puts it, "any blanket rejection of Freudian theory as a whole . . . simply flies in the face of the evidence" (p. 346). Recently, Fisher and Greenberg (1977) have concluded the same:

> . . . balancing the positive against the negative, we find that Freud has fared rather well. . . . One of the things we have most clearly verified is that it is possible to approach Freud's work in a scientific spirit. . . . We have been amused by the fact that while there is the stereotyped conviction widely current that Freud's thinking is not amenable to scientific appraisal, the quantity of research data pertinent to it that has accumulated in the literature grossly exceeds that available for most other personality or developmental theories. . . . (pp. 395–96)

Evidence obtained through commonly accepted scientific investigatory procedures has documented many psychoanalytic hypotheses such as the oedipus complex and sexual symbolism (Kline, 1972). The second and fourth objections concern the methodology of collecting data. The analyst is alone with the patient in the consulting room — without safeguards against misperceptions, avoidance of certain data, and suggestions to the patient which might corrupt the evidence. It must be realized, however, that in a sense psychoanalysis is a special kind of science which deals with subjective states, those of the analyst as well as those of the patient. There is an interplay between the patient's and the analyst's conscious mentation and unconscious fantasy. Such a special area of investigation demands special investigative methods. These entail subjectivity, but disciplined subjectivity. The use of free association allows subjective states to manifest themselves. To understand and to discover the unconscious, one needs both logic and fantasy. "The exactness of psychoanalysis is therefore not *the ambitious myth of minds* misled by the fantastic. It is the rational use of the psychoanalyst's fantasy to decipher the fantasy of the analysand" (Lagache's italics, 1966, p. 432). Psychoanalysts have now turned to the observation of infants to supplement the data obtained in the consulting room. Currently, each method, the laboratory "objective" investigations and the consulting room "subjective" explorations, provide a framework, boundaries, and checks and balances on the other.

There is another consideration. Recent research has hypothesized that we perceive the world according to our own individualities and that "at no level in our continuum of cognition is there any way to separate a 'subjective' from an 'objective' " (Holland, 1978). Thus, "one can *never* subtract out experimenter 'bias,' for that is, precisely, identity" (Holland's italics, 1978). Truth is in the process of apprehension and in consensual validation. "Knowledge is made by people, and not found" (Bleich, 1975, p. 319). A full exploration of this idea cannot be indulged in here, but if there is any "truth" in this subjectivist approach, the implications for science and the acquisition of all knowledge are great. However, it is psychoanalysis which can provide the guidelines for "scientific" explorations in this subjective context — for in the psychoanalytic situation, the mental states of the patient (object) and of the analyst (subject), as well as the interaction between them (process), are all considered (cf. Green, 1975, p. 104).

The third criticism, that psychoanalysis draws unscientific evidence from other fields, again misses the point that psychoanalysis is a special kind of science, one which concerns the understanding of man as a whole. (Even the "hard" natural sciences, such as physics and chemistry, draw on each other.) Psychoanalysis is not only concerned with the understanding of how mental acts and productions occur, but also with understanding why they occur (Wallerstein, 1974). Psychoanalysis is concerned with meaning and is a humanistic approach to man. In order to understand meaning, all man's activities such as myths, folktales, and art must be examined and drawn upon. As Eissler (1965) puts it:

> A psychological theory of the higher functions — such as creativity, or aesthetic or ethical sensibility — presupposes knowledge about what man creates, and what he regards as beautiful and ethical, and this again requires reference to the findings of the anthropic sciences. . . . The metapsychology of a historical process, of social institutions, of art, — in short, of all subjects of anthropic research — thus becomes conceivable. The basic general goal of psychoanalytic anthropic research would consequently be a *metapsychology of culture.*
> (Eissler's italics, p. 158)

If man is to be understood, culture must be understood; if psychoanalysis is to attempt to understand man, it must attempt to understand culture. It can only do that by drawing upon other humanistic fields (Mollinger, 1977), whether "unscientific" or not.

The fifth objection concerns the reliance of psychoanalysis on metaphoric thinking. What must be realized here is that all sciences in their beginnings depend on analogy and metaphor to construct theory. In fact, metaphor is a way to apprehend patterns and knowledge. Lacan (1966) holds that metaphor occurs at the precise point where sense comes out of non-sense. In the refinement of the metaphor comes, if we believe in objectivity, the approximation of reality. Metapsychological theories, which have been frequently regarded as too abstract and metaphorical, are logical artifacts which assist in ordering data. They cannot be proved or disproved by constructing empirical tests; if they are to be replaced it must be by theories which order the data better. Only at that time can we say that these "metaphors" can be eliminated. "Once it has achieved the status of paradigm, a scientific theory is declared invalid only if an alternate candidate is available to take its place. . . . To reject one paradigm without simultaneously substituting another is to reject science itself. That act reflects not on the paradigm but on the man." (Kuhn, 1962, pp. 76–79).

Turning to the popular perspective of psychoanalysis, we find misperception and misunderstanding. "No very significant developments have taken place . . . beyond the initial work of the master" (McCurdy, 1971, p. 116). Referring to the field of psychoanalysis and to its originator Sigmund Freud, this statement was made by a well-known psychologist in a leading psychological journal in 1971. Probably the most prevalent misconception today (which, as we see, is evident even in the scientific and psychological community) is that psychoanalysis equals Freud and that Freud equals psychoanalysis. Its implication is that a psychoanalyst necessarily believes every word that Freud wrote and that he supports every theory that Freud postulated. This notion is manifested daily in the question "are you a Freudian?" Other well-known manifestations of this misperception appear in the criticisms of the feminist movement against psychoanalysis. To most women in this movement, a psychoanalyst is one who believes women are inferior to men and belong in the home as housewives.

It must be recognized that a lot more has been said on the

subject of femininity since Freud's first theories. Such analysts as Karen Horney (1967) and Erik Erikson (1968) have been concerned with this issue. In the last couple of years, book after book has appeared containing new views by analysts such as Miller (1976) and Chasseguet-Smirgel (1970). A particularly noteworthy conception of basic issues in femininity is offered by Kestenberg (1975) who emphasizes the vulnerability of women to inner-genital sensations. Though I have not been able to go into this subject in this chapter, early psychoanalytic concepts about women, especially Freud's, have been under heavy debate by analysts since the early years of psychoanalysis.

Another manifestation of popular misconception is the assumption that psychoanalysts believe Freud's theory of the death instinct. This theory holds that there is an aspiration or drive toward death and that this drive is redirected from the self to others, thus producing aggression.

With regard to the death instinct, it is now clear that this theory is still controversial within the psychoanalytic community. Numerous other theories on the origin of aggression have been postulated. It is important to realize here that on this issue, and on others, more research and thought have occurred in psychoanalysis than Freud's.

Concepts of femininity and the death instinct are only two examples of well known problems. Psychoanalytic thought has been developed and expanded in many areas beyond Freud, as my preceding summary of psychoanalytic theory indicates. Whereas Freud was concerned with instinctual drives, as can be seen by the brief sketch of a child's early development, contemporary analysts have been more interested in the way we adapt to our families and our environment and the way we form our goals and values. There is Erikson's work (1968) on identity and the life-cycle, Hartmann's (1939) work on the ego's autonomous functions, and Jacobson's (1964) interest in the infant's early relation to the mother. As Guntrip (1971) has recently said, "Today the question to ask is not so much 'What did Freud say?' but 'What has Freud's work led to?' " (p. 5). Using this context, I have attempted in this summary to refer to the developments by others in the field of psychoanalysis, even though Freud may have provided the basic framework.

# 3/THE LITERARY SYMBOL:

# Wallace Stevens's Archetypal Hero

In approaching the literary symbol from a psychoanalytic perspective, one can choose between two traditional approaches, the Freudian and the Jungian. In so doing, one is also choosing to go in one of two directions, the personal or the supra-personal. For Freud, the symbol, having meaning that is personal to the creator of the symbol himself, is a direct equivalence of the individual's psychic state; it is influenced by his unconscious. The symbol is related to a personal fantasy whose function is to satisfy a wish, a wish which first appeared in childhood.

> Mental work is linked up to some current impression, some provoking occasion in the present which has been able to arouse one of the subject's major wishes. From there it harks back to a memory of an earlier experience (usually an infantile one) in which this wish was fulfilled; and it now creates a situation relating to the future which represents a fulfillment of the wish. What it thus creates is a day-dream or phantasy, which carries about it traces of its origin from the occasion which provoked it and from the memory. Thus past, present

and future are strung together, as it were, on the thread of the wish that runs through them. (Freud, 1908, pp. 147–48)

Art, for Freud, is a personal wish-fulfilling fantasy whose source is personal childhood experiences which remain in the personal unconscious. The symbol, deriving from the personal unconscious and the handling of the unconscious forces by the individual's ego becomes a personal sign referring back to childhood, to wishes, and to conflict.

For Jung, the creative situation is entirely different. He proposes that the "true" work of art goes beyond the personal concerns and limitations of the artist (Jung, 1922). The artistic material can be traced to the artist's childhood and relationship to his family. If it is, a confusion arises between neurosis and art. For Jung, such an exploration at best can broaden our knowledge of the psychological antecedents of a creative work, but it cannot help us in judging the work or in dealing with the work of art itself. For Jung, art is suprapersonal. The meaning of the art work is not a result of the artist's intention alone. Results of the artist's uncontrolled and unwilled creative impulse are thoughts and symbols which can only be apprehended intuitively. True symbols and images are not consciously created; they arise from the collective unconscious, the conveyor of archetypes and primordial images. The collective unconscious, archetypes, and primordial images all take us into a realm beyond the individual and beyond his personal unconscious:

> In contrast to the personal unconscious, which is a relatively thin layer immediately below the threshold of consciousness, the collective unconscious shows no tendency to become conscious under normal conditions, nor can it be brought back to recollection by any analytical technique, since it was never repressed or forgotten. The collective unconscious is not to be thought of as a self-subsistent entity; it is no more than a potentiality handed down to us from primordial times in the specific form of mnemonic images or inherited in the anatomical structure of the brain. There are no inborn ideas, but there are inborn possibilities of ideas that set bounds to even the

boldest fantasy and keep our fantasy activity within certain categories: *a priori* ideas as it were, the existence of which cannot be ascertained except from their effects. (Jung, 1922, pp. 80–81)

The collective unconscious, then, contains "natural ways of thinking, lines of least resistance, tendencies to gravitate in our ideas toward primitive modes of thought" (Mullahy, 1948, p. 149; cf. Snider, 1977a, 1977b). True symbols are expressions of these intuitive ideas and are not related to the personal unconscious. In the collective unconscious, manifestations of the archetypes, the symbols, are not derived from repressed personal wishes occurring in the artist's childhood.

Jung (1922) says it is these archetypes and true symbols which give great art its power: "That is the secret of great art, and of its effect upon us. The creative process, so far as we are able to follow it at all, consists in the unconscious activation of an archetypal image, and in elaborating and shaping this image into the finished work" (p. 82). These archetypes seize hold of the individual artist: "the creative power of the unconscious seizes upon the individual with autonomous force of an instinctual drive and takes possession of him without the least consideration for the individual, his life, his happiness, or his health" (Neumann, 1959, p. 98). From the Jungian perspective, the artist is mostly passive, a reacting subject to the collective unconscious, and he has a "preponderance of the archetypal" (Neumann, 1959). Once more, we see the personal deemphasized.

The artist does elaborate the archetypal image into the finished work. Using the artistic medium, colors, forms, words, the artist attempts to understand and assimilate the archetype which at first overwhelmed him (Neumann, 1959). The artist molds the archetype, not according to his own needs, but according to the needs of the community. Jung (1930) asserts that the archetypal symbols which appear in art are compensatory. They correct an imbalance: "Whenever conscious life becomes one-sided or adopts a false attitude, these images 'instinctively' rise to the surface in dreams and in the visions of artists and seers to restore the psychic balance, whether of the individual or of the epoch" (p. 104). In each particular historical period there is a dominant heritage of archetypes, the cultural canon. The creative artist manifests the "balancing" archetypes within the context of this heritage.

> The collective consciousness, the cultural canon, the system of the culture's supreme values toward which its education is oriented and which set their decisive stamp on the development of the individual consciousness. But side by side with this is the living substratum, the collective unconscious, in which new developments, transformations, revolutions, and renewals are at all times foreshadowed and prepared and whose perpetual eruptions prevent stagnation and death of a culture. (Neumann, 1959, p. 89)

Though these are new developments, they must be in a contemporary form, a form that "changes according to the time, the place, and the psychological constellation of the individual in whom they are manifested" (Neumann, 1959, p. 82). The archetype becomes synthesized into a specific, historical situation.

With its emphasis on symbolism, the Jungian approach to art is particularly applicable to the poetry of Wallace Stevens, a poet whose work appears comprehensible only after clarification of his images and symbols. Brief use of Jung's ideas has been made in clarifying images of the sun and woman in Stevens's work (Doggett, 1966; Kessler, 1972), but the most fertile symbol for a Jungian approach is Stevens's use of the hero or superman (Benamou, 1959). The image of the hero in Stevens's poetry can be seen as a Jungian "compensatory" symbol, molded by the poet into the language of the modern age but with recognizable similarities to previous manifestations of the archetypal hero.

Though Jung suggests, in contrast to the Freudians, that the artist's personal life is mostly irrelevant to his art, Stevens's conscious thoughts, recorded in his letters and essays at the time the heroic image first appeared and when it is developed later, show an apparent need for a compensatory image to correct an imbalance in attitude. The image of the hero first appears in "Owl's Clover" and in "The Man With the Blue Guitar" during the years 1936 and 1937. In the latter poem, the speaker describes the transcendent qualities of his hero: "I sing a hero's head, large eye/And bearded bronze, but not a man." Stevens's letters in previous years, 1933 and 1934 in particular, imply the need for an image of a positive ideal to counterbalance his pessimism. In a bitter and cynical mood, he is generally distressed by the Depression. He seems to be irritated by the disturbed conditions in Cuba, by the absurdity of going "to bed leaving the lights burning all over the house in order to fool the bums," and by watching Gertrude Stein's "Four Saints in Three Acts" with "numerous asses of the first water in the audience" (Stevens, 1966, pp. 266–67). In *Parts of a World* (1942) the image of the hero is the most pervasive one, appearing in such poems as "United Dames of America," "Asides on the Oboe," and "Examination of the Hero in a Time of War." "Asides on the Oboe," a poem whose main purpose is to state the need for a belief in the hero, was first published in December 1940. Possibly it reflects the necessity of an image to alleviate the effects of a series of personal problems the poet encountered during this time. In a letter to Henry Church, dated August 23, 1940, Stevens summarizes some of the factors which have brought on a defenseless and powerless mood:

> This has not been a good summer. My only brother died a month or two ago, and last week my wife's mother was killed in an automobile accident. This sort of thing, and the demnition [sic] news, added to the demnition grind at the office, makes me feel pretty much as a man must feel in a shelter waiting for bombing to start. (Stevens, 1966, pp. 364–65)

Just as Stevens's mood a decade earlier resulted from social as well as personal crises, his pessimism in the '40s was caused by more than personal problems. In an essay published the same year as *Parts of a World*, "The Noble Rider and the Sound of Words," Stevens is particularly concerned with what he calls the pressure of external reality, the war especially, but, in addition, a violent social atmosphere: "The war is only part of a war-like whole" (Stevens, 1951, p. 21). Many of the factors which led to the poet's "imbalanced" attitude during these years are impersonal in the Jungian sense that they were common to many people at the time. Disgusted with the world as he saw it, Stevens perceived a physically and spiritually violent world. To replace an attitude of fatalistic pessimism, he wants to create a foundation for a romantic optimism. Referring to the hero in a letter to Hi Simons dated August 29, 1940, he says that he is looking for a superman without weaknesses:

> If the future . . . also comes to nothing, sha'n't we be looking round for some one superhuman to put us together again, some prodigy capable of measuring sun and moon, someone who, if he is to dictate our fates, had better be inhuman, so that we shall know that he is without any of our weaknesses and cannot fail. (Stevens, 1966, pp. 371–72)

The image of the hero which appears during these years could arise both as a corrective for Stevens's one-sided mood and for the culture as a whole. It is interesting to note that Stevens himself would agree with the Jungian belief that art reflects the psychic needs of the culture and responds to cultural pressures: "To sum it up, the pressure of reality is, I think, the determining factor in the artistic character of an era" (Stevens, 1951, p. 21).

According to other statements by Stevens, these personal and social factors are not those which motivate his creation of the hero. His hero is meant to alleviate the crisis of belief occurring in the twentieth century. Both Jung and Stevens react to the prevalent lack of religious faith. In "The Undiscovered Self (Present and Future)" Jung (1957) proposes that modern man requires a religious symbol which expresses his needs to achieve a synthesis in life. Stevens rejects as outdated the gods of organized religion and the existence of any supernatural being, but unable to reconcile himself to man's lonely condition on earth he seeks a replacement for God. "If one no longer believes in God (as truth), it is not possible merely to disbelieve; it becomes necessary to believe in something else"

(Stevens, 1966, p. 370). For Stevens, disorder and chaos in the modern age result from the impossibility of belief in God, and the poet proposes the hero as a symbol of redemption. The image of the hero arises out of the crisis of belief in the early twentieth century. As Stevens puts it in "Examination of the Hero in a Time of War," "Unless we believe in the hero, what is there/To believe."

In order to ameliorate this crisis, Stevens formulates his heroic image in terms to which modern man can respond. As we have seen, for Jung, the creative process not only consists of the emergence of the archetypal image but also the shaping of this image by the artist into a form to which the culture can respond. "By giving it shape, the artist translates it into the language of the present, and so makes it possible for us to find our way back to the deepest springs of life" (Jung, 1922, p. 82). The particular form of the image must be appropriate to the particular age. Stevens realizes the same requirement. As he puts it in "Asides on the Oboe," a new, final belief must replace the obsolete fictions of the past. The poet's intention is to replace dead beliefs with a vital, new one, what he calls the supreme fiction: "If we are to think of a supreme fiction . . . we might choose to create it in the image of a man: an agreed-on superman" (Stevens, 1966). Recognizing that the twentieth century is a humanistic one, he calls it the era of the idea of man. Instead of creating an image of a transcendent God, Stevens presents a humanistic ideal (Mollinger, 1976). "A substitute for all the gods;/This self, not that gold self aloft" ("The Man With the Blue Guitar," Stevens, 1954).

In general the poet's definition of the hero is vague and abstract. From a Jungian perspective, this quality may be expected of an archetype.

> We would expect a strangeness of form and content, thoughts that can only be apprehended intuitively, a language pregnant with meanings, and images that are true symbols because they are the best possible expressions for something unknown — bridges thrown out towards an unseen shore. (Jung, 1922, pp. 75–76)

Arising as it does from the collective unconscious, the archetypal hero is necessarily vague. Stevens himself shows some
understanding of the origin of his symbol. In "Examination of
the Hero in a Time of War" he defines the hero as a feeling.
"There is no image of the hero./There is a feeling as definition." Where Jung says that the archetypes and mythological
heroes, coming from the unconscious, are projections of man's
being, Stevens similarly states that his symbol of the hero,
coming from feeling, is a projection of the poet's emotion.

> The hero is a feeling, as man seen
> As if the eye was an emotion,
> As if in seeing we saw our feeling
> In the object seen. . . .
> ("Examination of the Hero in a Time of War")

That archetypal heroes are projections of the self clarifies
Stevens's apparently paradoxical idea that we can have the
hero as an ideal and at the same time be him: "We have and
are the man." Stevens, in "Examination of the Hero in a Time
of War," is psychologically accurate regarding the true source
and phenomenological existence of the hero.

When Stevens does describe the hero with some specificity,
his imagery shows some similarity to that of previous world-
wide heroes (Campbell, 1949). The archetypal hero can appear as a warrior, slaying dragons and monsters. Stevens calls
his hero the "outer captain" in "A Thought Revolved." The
archetype is manifested as a lover who must perform a difficult task as a prerequisite to the bridal bed, as in the myth of
Cuchulainn. The hero of Stevens, portrayed as a lover in
"Like Decorations in a Nigger Cemetery" and "Asides on the
Oboe," appears again in "Examination of the Hero in a Time
of War" as a lover going to a special, secret rendezvous: "The
hero/Glides to his meeting like a lover. . . ." Just as the archetypal hero appears as an emperor, for example, Huang Ti, the
poet's hero is imagined as a queen and a dark-blue king in
"Extracts from Addresses to the Academy of Fine Ideas." The
archetype appears as a saint, Bodhisattva. Stevens's hero is
comparably embodied as a religious figure: "the inner saint,/

The pine, the pillar and the priest . . ." ("A Thought Revolved"). The general, typical manifestations of the archetypal hero seem to be manifested in Stevens' hero for the modern age.

Stevens's religious imagery of his hero is part of the idea of the archetypal hero. The function of Stevens's hero, like the function of the hero in general, is to redeem the world. The poet's religious terminology makes clear this redemptive trait. The hero is portrayed as Jesus Christ — as a communion, a golden "rescue," and bread and wine in "Examination of the Hero in a Time of War." He appears as a redeeming thought in "Extracts from Addresses to the Academy of Fine Ideas." The hero in general, appearing in mythology as Tammuz, Adonis, and Attis, redeems mankind by renewing life and by revitalizing the earth. Stevens implies that his hero has this same power of renewal by describing him as walking in dew and muttering milky lines in "Asides on the Oboe" and by calling him a "heavy-fruited star" in "A Thought Revolved." By reflecting the universe, the archetypal hero, the perfect microcosmic mirror of the macrocosm, brings peace to mankind: "he makes visible the repose and harmony of the central place" (p. 347). This statement by Campbell (1949) could be mistaken for one by Stevens, and much of Stevens's imagery becomes clear in the light of this general characteristic of the hero. The poet's hero is likewise all-encompassing. He is called a "human globe" in "Asides on the Oboe" and "man-sun, man-moon, man-earth, man-ocean" in "Examination of the Hero in a Time of War." The images of brilliance used by the poet, diamonds, crystals, mirrors, and glass, convey the hero's reflection of the universe. Through Stevens's hero, like the archetypal one, man can see the macrocosm and find repose. "He is the transparence of the place in which/He is and in his poems we find peace" ("Asides on the Oboe"). Since the hero in general is the microcosm, he also sums up all men. Otto Rank (1914) points out that this sum is both the total and the summit: "the hero should always be interpreted merely as the collective ego, which is equipped with all the excellences"

(p. 72). Describing the hero in "Asides on the Oboe" as a million diamonds which are the sum of mankind, Stevens then appropriately portrays his hero as both all men and as the ideal man. In "Examination of the Hero in a Time of War" the hero, fitting Rank's definition, is more explicitly the collective ego: "the hero is his nation/In him made one. . . ."

According to Campbell, the archetypal hero renews mankind by showing men the unity in multiplicity, the meaning of existence, the king within man, the eternal in the temporal, and, most importantly and in summation of the rest, the God in the human. Stevens's hero also manifests these traits. His hero in "Examination of the Hero in a Time of War" displays unity, "he is the heroic/Actor and act but not divided." Finally the hero is the supreme fiction in "Extracts from Addresses to the Academy of Fine Ideas," where he gives meaning to life: "The mass of meaning becomes composed again." Like the royal archetypal hero, in "A Thought Revolved," he embodies the higher qualities of man as the "son only of man and sun of men." For Campbell, seeing God in the hero teaches man to see God in himself and, in fact, to become God. The bodhisattva discloses "We in Him and He in Us" (p. 161). Like the archetypal hero, Stevens's hero is able to disclose God in man, "we project the idea of God into the idea of man" (Stevens, 1951), and, in bringing God to man, to redeem him.

Appropriately, when man feels the presence of the hero or sings hymns of the hero, he finds peace. In "Asides on the Oboe," oneness is attained when the hero is apprehended. In "Examination of the Hero in a Time of War," the same blissful unity is reached:

> To meditate the highest man,
>
> . . . . . . . . .
> Creates, in the blissfuller perceptions,
> What unisons create in music.

The goal of the hero is Nirvana, and the goal of the perceiver of the hero is to be a hero; therefore, Nirvana is the goal of whoever becomes aware of the hero. Stevens's hero is meant to lead us to Nirvana.

In his image of the hero, Stevens has reached into the collective unconscious to find a symbol to give life meaning in an age lacking solid religious beliefs. Since the age is generally skeptical of anything transcendent, the hero necessarily takes on a humanistic form. To compensate for a generally prevalent pessimism, the hero as ideal man appears as a symbol of romantic optimism. In its complex imagery, this symbol hints of the divine. The need for the incarnation of a divine image in times of despair and negation is, according to Campbell (1949), what the heroic myth satisfies: "The people yearn for some personality who in a world of twisted bodies and souls, will represent again the lines of the incarnate image" (p. 308).

# 4/THE LITERARY CHARACTER:

# Edgar Allan Poe's Roderick Usher

Though speculations on the relation of a literary character to its creator are, at times, unprovable, the actual analysis of a character as distinct from its author can be profitable. Other-worldly, strange, and suprahuman as they are, the characters in Edgar Allan Poe's tales sometimes are seen as "unreal": Ligeia returns from the dead; the narrator of "Berenice" removes Berenice's teeth while she lies in her grave; and Lackobreath in "Loss of Breath" is crushed, hung, and interred, but remains alive. Roderick Usher in "The Fall of the House of Usher" is also presented as wildly strange. Speaking of Usher's facial expression, the narrator cannot "connect its arabesque expression with any idea of simple humanity." But all these characters, though exaggerated, are human in some way. Psychoanalysis can help us understand how this is so, how particularly "unreal" characteristics are also particularly human ones. In "The Fall of the House of Usher" the narrator notes that Usher has "a mental disorder," "a peculiar temperament" and a "singular perversion," but what this malady is remains unclear. I shall argue in this chapter (1) that Usher can be seen as a depressed person, a generalization that unifies

many of the varied descriptions of him; (2) that the other
characters are reflections and mirrors for Usher's basic problems; (3) that he manifests typically depressive interactions
with others and typically depressive intrapsychic conflicts;
and (4) that an understanding of Usher leads to a better understanding of the themes of the story.

The manifest signs of depression can be grouped into four
categories: physical, behavioral, cognitive, and emotional
(Schuyler, 1974). Common physical signs are disorders in eating, weight loss, weakness, easy fatigability, and pain, all of
which Usher manifests. Having difficulty eating, "the most
insipid food was alone endurable," he loses weight and has
thin lips and emaciated fingers. He is weak and almost deadly
fatigued — a cadaverously wan, ghostly pallid, feeble invalid.
In addition, frequent reference is made to Usher's physical
pains, his bodily illness and his hypochondria.

Manifesting the physical signs of depression, Usher also
exhibits the behavioral ones, withdrawal, agitation, and almost complete self-involvement. "Sullen," "gazing upon va-
cancy," withdrawing completely from the outside world,
Usher's "reserve had been always excessive and habitual." His
sister has been "his sole companion for long years." He is
completely self-involved, almost to the point of a complete
disengagement from reality. His senses are oppressed, tortured, and horrified by odors, faint light, and most sounds. At
times incoherent, disordered, unorganized, and hurrying
with an "objectless step," Usher spends most of his time involved in his own wild imagination: his "elaborate fancy"
broods; his conceptions are "phantasmagoric"; his guitar per-
formances are of a "fantastic character"; and his poems, like
"The Haunted Palace," illustrate his "wild fantasias." In sum,
Usher exhibits "an excited and highly distempered ideality."
He is a man immersed in his own mind.

The cognitive, that is, the perceptual or intellectual, manifestations of depression, such as negative expectations for the
future, helplessness, hopelessness, and indecision, can be seen

in Usher as well. He pessimistically looks forward to his ultimate demise.

> "I shall perish," said he, "I *must* perish in this deplorable folly. Thus, thus, and not otherwise, shall I be lost. I dread the events of the future, not in themselves, but in their results."

Experiencing his own physical movements as "feeble and futile," he is helpless in affecting his future and his own well-being and despairs of finding a remedy for his malady. In the beginning of the story he reaches out for help from the narrator whom he summons to cheer him up. Within a few days, he falls again into despair. No one can help him for he *must* perish. Usher wanders with no object in mind, between indecision and empty decisiveness.

> His voice varied rapidly from a tremulous indecision (when the animal spirits seemed utterly in abeyance) to that species of energetic concision — that abrupt, weighty, unhurried, and hollow-sounding enunciation — that leaden, self-balanced and perfectly modulated guttural utterance — which may be observed in the lost drunkard, or the irreclaimable eater of opium, during the periods of his most intense excitement.

Displaying the emotional signs of depression, Usher is sad, anxious, angry. The House of Usher, symbolic of his mood, is a "mansion of gloom," "melancholy," "somber," and enveloped in an oppressive "atmosphere of sorrow." Within this "irredeemable gloom," Usher is overflowing with anxiety, a "bounden slave" to terror: "I have, indeed, no abhorrence of danger, except in its absolute effect — in terror. . . . I must abandon life and reason together, in some struggle with the grim phantasm, FEAR." Accompanying this sadness and anxiety are hints of an underlying anger. He is sullen, brooding, and bitter.

Usher manifests the physical signs of depression in his lack of appetite, loss of weight, weakness, and bodily pains; the behavioral signs in his withdrawal, agitation, and preoccupation with himself; the cognitive signs in his hopeless pessimism and helplessness; and the emotional signs in his sadness, anxiety, and anger. When the narrator appropriately labels the house "the melancholy House of Usher" and wants to alleviate "the melancholy of my friend," he unwittingly has made the correct diagnosis.

It has been pointed out that the House of Usher, including the surrounding countryside, the narrator, and his sister Madeline, are all reflections of Roderick Usher himself (Hoffman, 1972; Quinn, 1957). Being doubles of Usher, they all mirror his depressive features. Just as he is gloomy, the House and the countryside are dreary, desolate, melancholy, and dark. Approaching the House through the countryside, the narrator experiences an "utter depression of the soul" and an "unredeemed dreariness of thought," while Madeline is wasting away from apathy. When Usher is agitated, the weather becomes tempestuous and wild, and the vapors of the tarn become agitated. The House as well has a "wild inconsistency" in which the draperies are "tortured into motion," "swayed fitfully," and "rustled uneasily." Numerous times the narrator becomes "unnerved" and experiences "nervousness" and tremors. Madeline is seen "trembling." Usher's lifelessness is reflected in the tarn's "sluggishness," the House's lack of "vitality," the narrator's "feeble" actions, and Madeline's emaciation. Just as Usher fears "FEAR," the night is "wildly singular in its terror," the House is a "region of horror," and the narrator experiences "terror," "dread," "horror," and "wonder." Usher's anger and bitterness are also reflected: the waters of the tarn are "sullen," the air of the House is "stern," the narrator feels "bitterness," and Madeline's appearance exhibits "evidence of some bitter struggle." The depressive condition of Usher pervades the surroundings and the characters and is mirrored by them. No wonder then that when Madeline falls, Usher falls, and the House falls, all in Fall.

The mechanisms of such depressions have been variously explained, but it is generally agreed that a precipitating factor is the experience of loss: whether a lost loved one (Freud, 1917), a lost sense of self-esteem as, for example, from the loss of a job (Fenichel, 1945), or a loss of security (Bibring, 1953).

Once such an important loss occurs, specific reactions take place. First, rage is felt and directed at the lost person and then against the self. The image of the lost one is internalized in the person's psyche to compensate for the loss. The rage then attacks this internal image instead of the actual, lost external person (Freud, 1917). Secondly, guilt is experienced, first because of the rage and then because of a sense of responsibility for the loss. Finally, helplessness is felt as the person views the lost one as essential to his survival or self-esteem. As Bibring (1953) puts it, depression is a human way of reacting to frustration and misery whenever the ego finds itself in a state of (real or imaginary) helplessness against overwhelming odds. Depression then is an attempt to find a way to master rage, guilt, and helplessness.

The precipitating event of Usher's depression appears to be related to his sister Madeline, whose loss from death he is anticipating:

> He admitted, however, although with hesitation, that much of the peculiar gloom which thus afflicted him could be traced to a more natural and far more palpable origin — to the severe and long-continued illness, indeed to the evidently approaching dissolution, of a tenderly beloved sister. . . .

The importance of Madeline to Usher does not just center on their love, but also on the fact that she was his "sole companion for long years, his last and only relative on earth." When Madeline dies, Usher will be totally alone. Not only is he about to lose a loved one and the security of a constant companion, but also the world will soon see the demise of the House of Usher: " 'Her decease,' he said, with a bitterness which I can never forget, 'would leave him (him the hopeless and the frail) the last of the ancient race of the Ushers.' " The "time-honored" Usher race is, in Usher's eyes, about to end. He feels helpless to maintain it and the self-esteem based on being part of a long-lasting and honored family. He responds then to all three of the possible precipitating causes of depression: he is losing a loved one, a constant companion, and the esteem of being an Usher.

These losses induce a sense of helplessness and hopelessness, a feeling that he cannot cope on his own. As the narrator puts it, Usher is "the hopeless and the frail." Usher, thinking that he needs the help and care of another person more powerful than he is, is helpless and unloved without the other's presence and power. Since such emotions of helplessness and weakness are uncomfortable, there will be attempts to avoid feeling them. Like a patient who fills his day with numerous activities, compulsively going from work to social meetings to phone conversations, to avoid feeling sadness and despair, Usher in a sense does the same. To fill his time and escape his feelings, he either reads various abstruse works for hours on end or turns to the guitar:

> It was, perhaps, the narrow limits to which he thus confined himself upon the guitar, which gave birth, in great measure, to the fantastic character of his performances. But the fervid *facility* of his impromptus could not be so accounted for. They must have been, and were, in the notes, as well as in the words of his wild fantasias (for he not unfrequently accompanied himself with rhymed verbal improvisations), the result of that intense mental collectedness and concentration to which I have previously alluded as observable only in particular moments of the highest artificial excitement.

By "artificial," the narrator is referring to opium-taking, but he also is sensing the unreality of the excitement and the fact that it is disguising other feelings. Usher is manic at this point. As Winnicott (1935) puts it,

> in manic defense a relationship with the external object is used in the attempt to decrease the tension in inner reality. But it is characteristic of the manic defense that the individual is unable fully to believe in the liveliness that denies deadness. . . .(p. 131)

Even though he attempts to cope with his despair in his "fantasias" and artistic creations, internally Usher is empty. His voice is characterized by "abrupt, weighty, unhurried, and hollow-sounding enunciation." In his guitar playing, his intense feelings do finally break through when he gives his rendition of "The Haunted Palace" in which the palace, becoming discordant and chaotic, is a metaphor for his mind.

In attempts to handle helpless feelings, depressed people frequently come to therapy seeking help from a "powerful person," seeking "answers" from the analyst who, since he is a trained professional, "must" know them. The interaction becomes, in the patient's eyes, one between the incapable and the supercapable. Involved in a similar interaction with the narrator, Usher sends a letter requesting the narrator to come help him. "A letter, however, had lately reached me in a distant part of the country — a letter from him — which in its wildly importunate nature had admitted of no other than a personal reply." The word "importunate" conveys the insistent, demanding quality of the letter which *forces* the narrator to make a personal reply and coerces him into helping Usher — "with a view of attempting by the cheerfulness of my society, some alleviation of his malady." Usher, in fact, is saying "I am helpless; therefore, you must help me." The narrator responds:

> It was the manner in which all this, and much more, was said — it was the apparent *heart* that went with his request — which allowed me no room for hesitation; and I accordingly obeyed forthwith what I still considered a very singular summons.

Usher's emotional desperation, "heart," draws the narrator to him, but as the narrator senses, Usher is not asking for help, he is commanding it. The narrator knows the letter *admits* of "no other reply," he is "*allowed* . . . no room for hesitation" and the letter is a *summons*, which he must *obey* (my italics).

Upon his arrival the narrator is filled with pity, but Usher immediately makes clear what he expects from his visitor: "it was thus he spoke of the object of my visit, of his earnest desire to see me, and of the solace he expected me to afford him." Completely self-involved, Usher "entered, at some length, into what he conceived to be the nature of his malady." With his sympathy and concern expertly provoked by Usher, the narrator naturally attempts to be helpful. "I was busied in earnest endeavors to alleviate the melancholy of my friend."

Unfortunately, the narrator has fallen into a trap. In order to relieve his sense of helpless frustration, a depressed person often demands help and simultaneously rejects it. This provokes in the helper the same helpless frustration he himself is experiencing. A patient will demand a response from the analyst — "speak to me!" — but when the analyst does speak by asking a question or making an interpretation, the patient usually rejects the question as silly or the interpretation as obvious, incorrect, or hurtful. The patient wants to be given to, yet cannot accept what is given as sufficient. The narrator soon discovers this. "Bitterly did I perceive the futility of all attempt at cheering [his] mind" — and the narrator becomes helpless, hopeless, and angry, for he is being frustrated by a man who will not allow himself to be helped.

Just as the narrator becomes angry in his helplessness, so does Usher. Such anger builds from the frustration of being unable to change a situation and from the loss of contact with another person in this case. Sullen, bitter, and brooding, Usher is angry because of the expected loss of Madeline. " 'Her decease,' he said, with a bitterness which I can never forget, 'would leave him [sic] . . . the last of the ancient race.' " Usher is angry because of the position he is put in by the anticipated death of his sister. His bitterness about being the last of the family leads him to assume a somewhat self-centered perspective, even though one might suppose Madeline, being dead, will have the worst of it. But Usher is more than bitter, he is murderously enraged. He seems actually to commit murder by entombing his sister alive (Hoffman, 1972). This is no mere accident, for his artistic creations show that he is thinking of the vault long before he actually places Madeline in it.

> One of the phantasmagoric conceptions of my friend, partaking not so rigidly of the spirit of abstraction, may be shadowed

forth, although feebly in words. A small picture presented the interior of an immensely long and rectangular vault or tunnel. . . .

Before the entombment, Usher has painted a picture of the tomb. In addition, his verses, sung while he plays the guitar, also make clear that murder was on his mind.

> But evil things in robes of sorrow,
> Assailed the monarch's high estate;
> (Ah, let us mourn, for never morrow
> Shall dawn upon him, desolate!)
> And round about his home the glory
> That blushed and bloomed
> Is but a dim-remembered story
> Of the old time entombed.

The monarch's high estate is Usher's mind, which is full of sorrow because "the glory/That blushed" is "entombed" or actually will be entombed. The poem predates the actual entombment of the House's blushing glory, Madeline:

The disease which had thus entombed the lady in the maturity of youth, had left, as usual in all maladies of a strictly cataleptical character, the mockery of a faint *blush* upon the bosom and the face. . . . (my italics)

The verses tell us, for the truth will out, that Usher is not just sorrowful from the expected loss but also is assailed by "evil things in robes of sorrow." Sorrow covers up evil, that is, murder.

Entombment is an effort to cover up murder as well. Usher tells the narrator that the burial is imperative because "of certain obtrusive and eager inquiries on the part of the medical men." They might well be suspicious for, after all, Usher was singing funeral hymns and dirges even before the death of Madeline. Thinking the physician sinister, Usher is, in fact, projecting his own rage. The dynamic here is interesting. Either Usher is so furious at Madeline for her leaving him that he kills her, or, since she is about to leave him, and he feels he is driving her away (that is, killing her), he enacts in reality the fantasy that he is killing her.

Having fantasized murder and then committed it, Usher is plagued by guilt. After he puts his sister in the vault, the guilt becomes particularly burdensome. "I thought his unceasingly agitated mind was laboring with some oppressive secret, to divulge which he struggled for the necessary courage." The guilt pressures Usher to confess, which, of course, he finally does: "*I dared not speak! We have put her living in the tomb!*" This oppressive guilt weighs down Usher and all the characters even before the actual murder. In his letter to the narrator, he relates that it is a "mental disorder which *oppressed* him" (my italics). On first meeting the narrator, he explains that part of his malady is to experience the odors of the flowers as "oppressive." This oppressive mental disorder is, in part, the guilt from his murderous rage. If we look closely at the language which describes his malady, we can see intimations of guilt. The disease is described in curiously moral terminology. The narrator notes in Usher a "moral lack," "a want of moral energy," and Usher himself says he is suffering from a "constitutional and family evil." Echoed in the poem, this evil is seen as immorality disguised by sorrow: "evil things in robes of sorrow." The narrator makes clear that this evil pervades Usher's mind: "a mind from which darkness . . . poured forth upon all objects of the moral and physical universe, in one unceasing radiation of gloom." The evil and guilt in Usher pours forth and oppresses the narrator, makes the House and the surrounding countryside oppressive, and, of course, enters Madeline's vault and gives it an "oppressive atmosphere." It is this extreme guilt which gives Usher the sense that he "*must* perish in this deplorable folly."

Guilt over murder entails punishment, so Madeline returns. "Is she not hurrying to upbraid me for my haste?" The retribution for Usher's murderous impulses is death; when Madeline returns, Usher dies. Murder becomes suicide as Usher's guilt exacts its due. Since Usher's and Madeline's identities are merged (they are identical twins and their diseases are the same) in killing Madeline, Usher also is killing himself.

> For a moment she remained trembling and reeling to and fro
> upon the threshold — then, with a low moaning cry, fell heav-
> ily inward upon the person of her brother, and, in her violent
> and now final death agonies, bore him to the floor a corpse,
> and a victim to the terrors he had anticipated.

In their dying together, he kills her and she kills him. But, of
course, they were as good as dead already — she being catalep-
tic (simulating the outward signs of death) and he being a
"cadaver." The end of the story is the climax of this process,
the slow but steady emergence of Usher's murderous rage.
The rage leads to murder, suicide, and insanity, a schizophrenic process:

> the deterioration of the ego . . . may advance to the point
> where the ego is overwhelmed by destructive forces, and the
> patient, going from a depressive into an excited catatonic
> state, becomes manifestly homocidal or suicidal, or both. (Ja-
> cobson, 1966, p. 516)

This is precisely what happens in "The Fall of the House of
Usher." Usher dies, Madeline dies, and the House, symbolic of
Usher's mind, collapses. The lifting of Usher's depression is
described as the emergence of a "mad hilarity," a "hysteria," a
"wild vivacity." Finally Usher withdraws into a catatonic
state:

> The measured rocking movement of Usher was undisturbed. I
> rushed to the chair in which he sat. His eyes were bent fixedly
> before him, and throughout his whole countenance there
> reigned a stony rigidity.

Losing contact with reality, Usher has become immersed in
the primary process and his unconscious impulses. Fittingly,
Usher and his House descend into the deep and dark tarn, an
image for the murky unconscious processes which are manifested throughout the story.

To perceive Usher as depressed unifies the varied descriptions of him and of his doubles: the narrator, Madeline, and
the House. The typical depressive maneuvers he acts out and
the depressive mechanisms of his psyche provide us with a

framework which clarifies the plot and the development of the story. Fearing an expected loss, Usher becomes depressed. In his helplessness, he reaches out for help to the narrator but he rejects the help when it is offered. His rage at Madeline builds until, in fact, he does become responsible for the loss he fears by killing her. As his psyche collapses under the pressure of his destructive impulses, he suicidally provokes his own death and symbolically kills himself by killing Madeline, his double. The story is a journey into the psyche, but a specific psyche, the depressed one.

# 5/THE LITERARY WORK:

# Herman Melville's
# "Bartleby the Scrivener:
# A Story of Wall Street"

In Melville's "Bartleby the Scrivener: A Story of Wall Street" Bartleby's lack of motivation to work, his employer's motivation for putting up with him, the imagery, and even the actual subject of the story have yet to be fully clarified. The characters have been seen either as doubles of each other or as opposites, while the theme has been looked at from a social perspective or related to the biography of the author. A study of the story's imagery clarifies both the personalities of the characters and the theme. The characters' personal and interpersonal dynamics show us the subject of the story which is a unified literary work displaying a complex intertwining of theme, character, and imagery.

To eat or not to eat is the question which reverberates throughout the story and in the minds of the characters (cf. Miller, 1975). "Bartleby the Scrivener" is a feast of food in which all the characters partake. Smelling of eating-houses and spending his money on drink, the lawyer's old helper, Turkey, is described by metaphors of food: as a horse feels his oats, Turkey feels the coat that the lawyer had given him, and it makes him rash and restive. The younger helper, Nippers, is equally self-indulgent with food. Always suffering from indigestion, he nevertheless continues to feed himself gingernuts, cakes, and apples. He does not need to drink, as Turkey does, because "nature herself seemed to have been his vintner, and at his birth charged him so thoroughly with an irritable, brandy-like disposition, that all subsequent potations were needless." Ginger Nut, the twelve-year-old boy, not only brings back food for the others but supplies himself with various sorts of nuts. It is clear that all three helpers are involved with food, so much so that they *are* food, as their names tell us: Turkey, Nippers (as in, to take a nip), and Ginger Nut.

Just as their mouths are their most important bodily part, "my two scriveners were fain to moisten their mouths very often with Spitzenbergs," the narrator-lawyer, their employer, is a man of the mouth. Instead of food, he digests words:

> I was not unemployed in my profession by the late John Jacob Astor; a name which, I admit, I love to repeat, for it hath a rounded and orbicular sound to it, and rings like unto bullion.

Though not with Spitzenbergs, he too moistens his mouth, nor does he hesitate to interrupt his work for his dinner hour.

Whereas Turkey, Nippers, Ginger Nut, and the lawyer are all well fed, some to the point of indigestion, Bartleby is not. The lawyer notices that Bartleby never goes to dinner and, in fact, barely eats or drinks.

> I was quite sure he never visited any refectory or eating-house; while his pale face clearly indicated that he never drank beer like Turkey, or tea and coffee even, like other men. . . .

In the end he dies from starvation, even though the suitably named prison grubman, Mr. Cutlets, attempts futilely to feed him.

The continual emphasis on food and eating indicates that this story is not just about life on Wall Street but is also about something much more basic. So, too, do the names of the characters: Turkey, Nippers, Ginger Nut, Mr. Cutlets, and even Bartleby, which Murray (1965) suggests refers to "bottle baby." In fact, food submerges, and merges with the work being done in the law office. Turkey seals a mortgage with a ginger cake, and Ginger Nut's perspective on his job is similarly confused with food, especially his collection of nuts. "Indeed, to this quick-witted youth the whole noble science of the law was contained in a nut-shell." The work routine of the law office was organized around the assistants' eating habits. Nippers, suffering from indigestion, does not do much work in the morning, but he recovers enough by the afternoon to do some labor. Turkey works well in the morning but, after dining and drinking at noon, accomplishes no work later. For Bartleby too, working and eating are confused. Upon being hired, he immediately and enthusiastically dives into copying.

> At first Bartleby did an extraordinary quantity of writing. As if long famished for something to copy, he seemed to gorge himself on my documents. There was no pause for digestion.

Hungry for work, he almost uncontrollably stuffs it in.

Life, then, on Wall Street becomes eating on Wall Street, and the story no longer seems to be just sociological but also psychological. The characters in the story are hungry; this fact gives meaning to their relationships which draw on a psychological, developmental stage of early childhood.

At this early childhood level, as Erikson (1950) puts it, one lives through and loves (as well as hates) with his mouth. In terms of the child's relationship with another person, the child experiences the other person as a fulfiller of needs like his mother. The mother has no separate life of her own and exists only to feed him.

If one accepts that the characters in "Bartleby the Scrivener" evidence a peculiar amount of interest in food, it should not be surprising to find that what interests them most is the satisfaction of their needs. Turkey, indisposed after eating his dinner, not only does not work well for his employer in the afternoon but actually ruins much of what he does work on. Asked to take the afternoons off by the lawyer, he refuses and insists on staying, regardless of his employer's wishes. Nippers only puts in a half day's good work for a full day's pay and even usurps some of the lawyer's professional affairs.

Both of them are symbiotically "living off" the lawyer; he feeds them full pay, while they give back much less — and, in fact, "giving and taking" is the essence of all relationships in the story. The lawyer gives Turkey an old coat, while Turkey defends the status of their relationship by noting that he has supplied his employer some stationery. "With submission, sir, it was generous of me to find you in stationery on my own account." Described as a "piratical looking young man," his fellow worker Nippers is one who appears to take if not to steal. Ginger Nut functions as a fulfiller of needs, especially in "his duty as cake and apple purveyor for Turkey and Nippers."

Since his approach to life is basically the same, the lawyer wants his needs gratified in the easiest way. This attitude affects his life, as well as his job. "I am a man who, from his youth upward, has been filled with a profound conviction that the easiest way of life is the best." Being unambitious, the lawyer is only looking for work enough to feed him and make it easier for him to live. Counting on his appointment as a Master in Chancery to provide him eternal funds, he wanted to literally live off the appointment. "I had counted upon a life-lease of the profits." He views other people only in terms of what they can do for him and sees both Nippers and Turkey as "useful" to him. Upon first seeing Bartleby, he calls him a "valuable acquisition."

Although the lawyer does take from others, as they do from him, he functions mainly to feed others. He gives Turkey the coat; he continually hands money to Bartleby. His relationship to Bartleby becomes almost parental. The lawyer supports him monetarily, gives him a place to live, tries to protect him from others, feeds him through the grub-man, and even offers to take him home. The lawyer, half-seriously, begins to believe that his only role in life is to fulfill Bartleby's needs.

Gradually I slid into the persuasion that these troubles of mine, touching the scrivener, had been all predestined from

eternity, and Bartleby was billeted upon me for some mysterious purpose of an all-wise Providence. . . . Others may have
loftier parts to enact; but my mission in this world, Bartleby, is
to furnish you with office room for such period as you may see
fit to remain.

The lawyer is here, functioning as the good mother who supplies what is needed, exactly the kind of relationship that
Bartleby wants.

Pallid, sedate, forlorn, and melancholy, Bartleby is depressed, depressed from lack of food. First attacking his new
job because he is famished, he then attempts to manipulate
people to meet his needs. Ginger Nut brings him cakes, but
that is not enough. Soon the lawyer is expected to provide him
with room and board. Bartleby wants to be allowed to stay in
the law office, or rather live in the law office, without doing
any work. After all, a baby is not expected to work in order to
be fed by his mother. Bartleby prefers to be taken care of,
prefers to not work for love, prefers to have a loving parent
catering to his needs. Realizing this, the lawyer notes that "he
prefers to cling. . . ."

Unfortunately, having been starved for so long, Bartleby
can no longer be nourished by what he eats. Gorging himself
on his work does not sustain him. In the end, giving up copying, he stops working altogether. Soon real food nourishes
him as little as symbolic food. Never dining, "I am unused to
dinners," Bartleby "eats nothing but ginger nuts," but even
these are worthless. "Ginger, then, had no effect upon
Bartleby." For Bartleby, it really made no sense to take
money from the lawyer, food from the grub-man, Mr. Cutlets, or to go home with the lawyer. Wanting to be fed,
Bartleby is in hopeless despair of ever receiving anything
nourishing. Seeking the good mother, he finds only the bad, a
predicament symbolized by his previous job in the Dead Letter office:

Dead letters! does it not sound like dead men? Conceive a man
by nature and misfortune prone to a pallid hopelessness: can
any business seem more fitted to heighten it than that of con-

tinually handling these dead letters, and assorting them for the flames? For by the cartload they are annually burned. Sometimes from out the folded paper the pale clerk takes a ring: the finger it was meant for, perhaps, moulders in the grave; a banknote sent in swiftest charity: — he whom it would relieve, nor eats nor hungers any more; pardon for those who died despairing. . . .

Despair for food leads to a hopeless "dead" man.

As well as being depressed, Bartleby is also angry, angry at being deprived. In part, his anger comes out in an oral way in his giving everyone the "silent treatment." "I remembered that he never spoke but to answer." It shows, too, in his negativity; when he does answer, it is always with a "no" or a "I'd prefer not to." Continually repeating this statement, Bartleby is appropriately referred to as "mulish" and stubborn by the others. They also see him as full of disdain and haughtiness. Though Bartleby does not realize how provocative he is, the others are indeed provoked. Turkey, for example, wants to fight him physically. It is the lawyer who is most affected by feeling the impact of Bartleby's maneuvers. "Nothing so aggravates an earnest person as a passive resistance." Feeling "twinges of an impotent rebellion" and "disarmed," the lawyer is castrated by Bartleby, "For I consider that one, for the time, is in a way unmanned when he tranquilly permits his hired clerk to dictate to him, and order him away from his own premises."

Bartleby's aggression is not only a way to coerce the gratification he longs for, it is also a reaction to the deprivation of that gratification. Thinking of Bartleby's melancholy, the lawyer realizes that "the scrivener's pale form appeared to me laid out, among uncaring strangers, in its shivering winding sheet," and he wants to protect him, shield him from "rude persecution." Uncared for, Bartleby is dead, first symbolically and then actually; yet, Bartleby is also suicidal. Hating the depriving other, he kills himself to make the other person suffer. The lawyer, who is continually upset about him, is provoked to do more and more for him even in the face of rejection. Finally taken to the tombs, Bartleby blames the lawyer and angrily distrusts him. Since trust in the world develops from trust in the mother to feed one, and since this is a trust which Bartleby does not have, he turns on the lawyer. " 'I know you,' he said, without looking round, — 'and I want nothing to say to you.' " Bartleby, betrayed by being uncared for, angrily and suicidally rejects all help and starves himself to death (cf. Miller, 1975).

The other characters experience that anger which is intimately connected to the need-fulfilling relationships they have established. This anger comes from needing someone, from being frustrated, or from having to appease the other person to receive from him. "Disposed, upon provocation, to be slightly rash with his tongue," Turkey, from the lawyer's perspective, feeds himself, or has been fed, too much. Rash with his tongue after his meal, he becomes even more insolent on receiving a gift, a coat from the lawyer:

> One winter day I presented Turkey with a highly-respectable looking coat. . . . I thought Turkey would appreciate the favour, and abate his rashness and obstreperousness of afternoons. But no. I verily believe that buttoning himself up in so downy and blanket-like a coat had a pernicious effect upon him; upon the same principle that too much oats are bad for horses. In fact, precisely as a rash, restive horse is said to feel his oats, so Turkey felt his coat. It made him insolent. He was a man whom prosperity harmed.

Thinking that feeding Turkey will mellow him, the lawyer discovers the opposite: like an overfed horse, Turkey becomes irritable. For Turkey, it seems that too much food is an intrusion to be fought off; he is "pugilistic" and images himself a military leader attacking the documents he works on.

Nippers' aggression also comes out of his mouth and is apparently caused by indigestion:

> The indigestion seemed betokened in an occasional nervous testiness and grinning irritability, causing the teeth to audibly grind together over mistakes committed in copying; unnecessary maledictions, hissed, rather than spoken, in the heat of business. . . .

Whereas Turkey becomes combative after drinking, Nippers, with his brandy-like disposition, well fed by the vintner Nature at birth, does not need any further drink to be irritable and curse.

Whereas both Turkey and Nippers become orally aggressive after having been well fed, the lawyer's aggression is related to food in a different way. Telling us that he seldom loses his temper and that he is a "man of peace," he prides himself on the fact that he engages in "no vulgar bullying, no bravado of any sort, no choleric hectoring. . . ." However, he does become resentful and angry when his needs are not being met. He becomes rash when he discovers that he will not have a life-long income for the Chancery to live off. He wants to expel Turkey because he does not work well in the afternoon. When Bartleby stops contributing to the office, the lawyer becomes more and more resentful and desires to eliminate him. His rage seems to operate on the principle "if you will not give to me, I will remove you." He wants to "thrust [Bartleby] ignominiously from my presence" and "violently . . . from the premises." Trying always to control this anger, he forgets the matter or, having fantasies of murder, he strives "to drown my exasperated feelings toward the scrivener by benevolently construing his conduct."

Again, this is a particularly oral rage, a rage at not being fed, at not having needs met, which comes out in the lawyer's continual ironic tone and in his fantasies of cursing at Bartleby. More importantly, it is the way the lawyer holds in his aggression: he feeds himself. After being disobeyed again, the lawyer begins to become angry.

> "Very good, Bartleby," said I, in a quiet sort of serenely severe self-possessed tone, intimating the unalterable purpose of some terrible retribution very close at hand. At the moment I half intended something of the kind. But upon the whole, as it was drawing towards my dinner-hour, I thought it best to put on my hat and walk home for the day. . . .

His dinner puts a stop to acting out his aggressive feelings. Here we see how the ingestion of food works in an opposite direction than it does with Turkey and Nippers. They become more distempered after eating and drinking. The lawyer's aggression is similar to Bartleby's; both become angry over deprivation. The lawyer, however, knows how to feed himself, while Bartleby starves himself even more. He joins the depriver by depriving himself.

In such symbiotic need-fulfilling relationships, there are usually attempts at separation. For, even though one has his needs satisfied, when one is merged with another person, one loses self-identity, or the sense of self. To have a complete self, one must function independently. Turkey and Nippers, both well fed, if not overfed, spend half the day having their desires gratified and fulfilling the employer's needs. The other half a day, they are themselves — aggressive (Turkey) and ambitious (Nippers). They have partially separated from a symbiotic relationship in the direction of their individual development. Bartleby, because his need is so great, cannot separate at all. While his extreme hunger leads him to gorge himself, his extreme distrust prevents him from finding nourishment. He is caught in the dilemma of forever seeking and never finding, he wants help but cannot accept it. To be on his own is dangerous, since his is a world of uncaring strangers and rude persecution: "I thought I saw peering out upon him the eyes of murderers and thieves."

The lawyer's dilemma is different. Wanting to be rid of Bartleby, that is, to be on his own, he also wants to be with Bartleby, that is, symbiotically together. He fantasizes throwing the scrivener out; he moves his office away from him; he deserts him at the end. The lawyer has difficulty in even having fantasies about leaving Bartleby; he must constantly fight himself to create them. Thinking of confronting Bartleby, he feels that he is indulging an "evil impulse." Becoming resentful, he recalls the divine injunction "that ye love one another." For the lawyer, hate and separation are evil and forbidden.

The lawyer's negative view of separation, seeing it as an immoral abandonment of another human being, partially explains his difficulty in kicking the nonworking scrivener out. In addition, the lawyer benefits from his bond with Bartleby, for, as he says, Bartleby is useful and valuable to him. Though Bartleby is a "millstone," an affliction, a haunting apparition which produces melancholy in the lawyer, it is a "fraternal melancholy" caused in both of them by a deprivation of needs. It is the lawyer's own need which causes him to allow Bartleby to cling to him. In mothering, feeding, and caring for the scrivener, the lawyer is mothering himself. For all his rationalizations, he identifies with Bartleby and feeds him as he himself wishes to be fed:

> He is useful to me. I can get along with him. If I turn him away, the chances are he will fall in with some less indulgent employer, and then he will be rudely treated, and perhaps driven forth miserably to starve. Yes. Here I can cheaply purchase a delicious self-approval. To befriend Bartleby; to humour him in his strange wilfulness, will cost me little or nothing, while I lay up in my soul what will eventually prove a sweet morsel for my conscience.

The image of food, that delicious, sweet morsel, is revealing: in feeding the other person, he feeds himself. The lawyer is almost as involved in the symbiotic need-fulfilling relationship as Bartleby is. This is why he has such difficulty in breaking it up, a difficulty foreshadowed by his futile attempt to make Turkey take the afternoons off. Unfortunately, by fooling himself into thinking that the cost of these attachments is small, the lawyer sacrifices his identity. He becomes the victim of his surroundings. His colleagues laugh at him and gossip about him; he is driven from his office, and his employees rebel.

Since most of the characters are ambivalent over their needs, their other attributes are defenses against these symbiotic relationships. Describing himself as a safe, prudent man who keeps away from people, the lawyer never addresses a jury, never seeks public applause. Rather, he hides himself away among legal documents, "in the cool tranquillity of a snug retreat, do a snug business among rich men's bonds and mortgages and title-deeds." Emotionally aloof, he chats

about sentimental stories and admits that his first experience
of melancholy, in sixty years of life, was caused by Bartleby.
His organizational thoroughness and his capacity to distance
himself and objectify himself results in him thinking of himself as a legal document. "*Imprimus:* I am a man who. . . ."
This aloofness and distancing are meant to avoid invasions of
himself. Speaking of the turbulence of the law profession, he
states "yet nothing of that sort have I ever suffered to invade
my peace." Yet, when Bartleby arrives his peace is invaded,
first by Bartleby's symbiotic clinging and angry rebellion and
then by the lawyer's own needs to mother and cling. Bartleby
has such a strong effect on the lawyer because he has forced
him after sixty years to experience needs and frustrations the
lawyer has avoided throughout his whole life. When in his
closing statement the lawyer speaks of starvation and despair
and sighs "Ah Bartleby! Ah humanity!" he actually means
"poor Bartleby and poor me."

Bartleby is even more aloof. Seeking solitude, Bartleby is
constantly in his "hermitage," his work area. By neither eating, talking, working, looking at the lawyer, nor giving, he
refuses to relate to others. Declining to join the group of Turkey, Nippers, Ginger Nut, and the lawyer, he symbolically
makes clear his refusal to join humanity. The lawyer concludes that there is nothing "ordinarily human about
him. . . ." Almost autistic, Bartleby's withdrawal from
others is more severe than the lawyer's. He stares at the wall
and day-dreams in his hermitage. Later, in the Tombs, he
faces the "dead-wall" until he dies in a fetal position, the
ultimate snug retreat. Like the lawyer, he, too, is attempting
to prevent the invasion of his self by others, with all the emotional involvement that entails. He stands as "a perpetual
sentry in the corner" forever, "without moving from his privacy." His first refusal to work is to fend off a demand which
intrudes upon this privacy, but Bartleby's withdrawal is also a
denial of his own needs. Not unexpectedly, this results in his
death.

In summary, we have moved from an examination of the
predominant oral imagery in the story to an understanding of

the interpersonal dynamics of the characters. We are presented with a continuum of characters all involved in symbiotic, need-gratifying relationships. These relationships are founded on basic wishes, as Bartleby's favorite word "prefer" indicates. At one end of the continuum are Turkey and Nippers, who have been well nurtured, perhaps too well nurtured, and for whom more food means engulfment by the world. For at least half the day, they attempt to move on and develop their own selves, Turkey by being aggressive and Nippers by being ambitious. At the other end of the continuum are the lawyer and Bartleby. Still longing for nurturance, the life-lease of easy gratification, the lawyer attempts to deny this desire by staying aloof from others and by controlling his emotions. When he does become involved, he denies his need by fulfilling it vicariously—he mothers instead of being mothered. Whereas the lawyer has at least partially found the easy way of life, Bartleby has never found it. Apparently never having been fed, he is famished. Since he cannot trust what is given to him, he autistically withdraws and creates his own world. In this ultimate despair, and angry because of betrayal by others, he gives up and kills himself.

Given the similarities in their characters, it is no wonder that critics vacillate between considering the lawyer or Bartleby more important. As some have pointed out, they are "doubles" of each other, and so indeed in their need, their anger, and their "fraternal melancholy," they are. In symbiotic relationships, there is no clear distinction between the self and the other person. There is rather a fusion of the internal images of the self and the other person. Only when one has become one's self is there differentiation. The story certainly is not just about Wall Street. It is about basic needs, the symbiotic ways these needs are fulfilled, and the anger, distrust, and despair which results when they are not met (cf. Miller, 1975). It concerns dependence on others for gratification, the loss of the self in such dependent relationships, the quest for the self in independence, and the defenses used to avoid acknowledging these complex feelings.

# Unifying Symbols: Sylvia Plath's Poetry

The intense emotion of Sylvia Plath's difficult poetry grips us, but the obscure imagery befuddles us at times. Being personal, the poetry draws out our empathy. In being too personal, it conceals its meaning. The strange and unusual references of Plath's images can be disentangled and made somewhat more comprehensible by the use of a psychoanalytic perspective.

Sylvia Plath was a poet; Sylvia Plath committed suicide. To separate these two facts is impossible. Just as death obsessed her mind, images of death pervade her poetry. In his introduction to the 1966 edition of *Ariel* (Plath, 1966), Robert Lowell notes that the death which seems continually to haunt Sylvia Plath in her poetry appears in unexpected and unusual images. As he points out, both the birthday present she receives and the lover who seeks her are symbols for death. These two images are not simply isolated instances of Plath's morbid concern but exemplify the large complex of death imagery which pervades her poetry. Including both traditional symbols and more personal and individual ones, this complex consists of the sea; the color black with associated grey and shadow; coldness in the form of ice and snow; stone and the related image of marble statues; the machine or engine, usually in the form of a railroad train; and, finally, serpents and snakes (cf. Lavers, 1966, and Lucie-Smith, 1966). Appearing in conjunction with each other, these images reinforce the significance and meaning of each other. Appearing alone, each calls to mind its associations with the others. For example, cold is employed so frequently in conjunction with the sea that when the symbol is used alone it forces the reader to think of the sea also. An analysis of the consistent symbolic use of these images is helpful in the explication of seemingly obscure poems. For instance, "Private Ground" at first reading seems to be about the speaker's rescue of a dying fish. The poem makes use of such symbols as frost, marble statues, and machines and thereby reveals its concern with the speaker's own death, figuratively if not literally (Mollinger, 1975).

Close observation of this complex of death symbolism can reveal not only the connection between seemingly disparate images, but the central operative force behind them, the very force which causes them to be so haunting, so pervasive, and so obsessive. It is difficult to discern immediately how these single images relate to each other. How, for instance, is a snake associated with an engine? How do stones relate to the sea? As will become clear in the course of this analysis, the unifying concept relating the individual images to each other is the figure of the father. Behind any image of death lies the father; where death is, there also is the father. As the speaker in "The Colossus" says, the father is the "mouthpiece of the dead." The key "father poems" in each of Plath's major volumes present, almost as if in summary, many of the connections between her images. "Man in Black" in *The Colossus* (1957) associates the father with the sea, blackness, greyness, ice, rock, stones, and the machine. "Daddy" in *Ariel* (1966) connects him with blackness, greyness, a marble statue, the Atlantic sea, trains, and snow. These connections are pervasive throughout the poetry, and the connection between death and father clarifies the appropriateness of the individual images of death. Blackness needs no subtle justification as a symbol of death; however, the logical or associative connection between death and the serpent or the machine is not immediately clear. It shall be seen that the father is the element which makes Plath's use of these symbols both clear and meaningful. As an analysis of "Totem" will show, some of Plath's poems will only yield their meaning when these symbolic connections are understood.

The sea or water is the most pervasive image of death in the poetry. Poem after poem in *The Colossus* portrays the sea overwhelming man's defenses against it. In "Point Shirley" the waves leap over the seawall, and in "The Bull of Bendylaw" the sea, imaged as a bull, bucks at the garden gate and breaks through it. The image is used just as extensively in *Ariel*: in "Paralytic" water enwraps the speaker's head in smothering cellophane. Since from a psychological viewpoint water can be interpreted as symbol of the mother's womb, the sea can be appropriately employed to represent death. In Plath's images the womb and the tomb are in association. In seeking a watery death, Plath's personas seek both the original source of life and the confinement of death. Though the sea is frequently related to the mother, the poet, using the more general connotations of the sea as death, clearly connects it with the father. In "Man in Black," the father figure strides before the sea's waves; in "Daddy" the speaker sees her father's head in "the freakish Atlantic"; and in "Full Fathom Five" the father is an old man beneath the sea.

Plath's more obscure sea imagery can now be clarified. Imaging the sea as a knife in "A Winter Ship," as an arrow in "The Colossus," and as a bull in "The Bull of Bendylaw," Plath brings together the sea and obvious symbols of masculinity. Psychoanalytically, all these symbols can represent the phallic aggressive qualities of a man. Even when the father is not explicitly associated with the sea, his presence is implicit in the figurative language used to describe it (cf. Orgel, 1974).

Black is accepted as a symbol of death both consciously –

mourners wear black — and unconsciously in dreams. From Plath's early poem "Two Views of a Cadaver Room," in which the speaker sees four men "black as burnt turkey" in a dissecting room, to her late poem "Little Fugue," in which death is imaged as a black tree, this symbol pervades the poems. Plath adds the father to black's symbolic meaning. As Lucie-Smith (1966) correctly notes, the man in the black coat and black shoes in "Man in Black" is similar to the father in "Daddy" who is called a black man with a black heart. With the symbolism of blackness revealed, it can now be seen that the father appears implicitly in more poems than would at first be expected. The four black, male cadavers in "Two Views of a Cadaver Room" refer to the father. More fertile possibilities lie in later poems, where again symbols of masculinity in general connect the father to the image. In "Little Fugue" the poet uses numerous images of death, cold and black, and explicitly identifies the father with both blackness and a yew tree, another traditional symbol of death. "I see your voice/Black and leafy. . . ." This identification of a male relative with a tree is not unusual, since trees can be associated with family trees and with the male sexual organ. As Gutheil (1951) puts it, "Phallic symbolism is inherent in the picture of a *tree* (Tree of Life)" (p. 141). The use of the symbol of the yew tree in "Little Fugue" and knowledge of the connections between the father, death, and blackness, somewhat clarifies "The Moon and the Yew Tree." This poem, like "Little Fugue," employs several images of death: cold, black, mists, clouds, sea. When the speaker says that "the message of the yew tree is blackness," the reader can interpret the line as figuratively connecting the father and death. Part of what haunts the speaker in this poem, put variously, is the death of her father, her dead father, or a suicidal wish somehow connected with her father: "The trees of the mind are black."

The color grey, related to black and associated with the sea in the poetry, also connotes death. In "Point Shirley" of *The Colossus*, the destructive sea is portrayed by grey waves. In "Wuthering Heights," the grey sheep and the grey weather tempt the speaker to give up life. Grey is associated with haunting and masculine figures which seem, at times, to hint strongly of the father. In "The Thin People," grey people terrify the speaker, and at one point they are connected, perhaps unconsciously, with the father. The speaker refers to their "kingship," a symbol which, if it appears in a dream or in the unconscious, can be representative of the father.

One of my patients, a young man, had the following dream about me:

> You were sitting behind a desk with short hair. You told me to stop going to the homosexual baths or stop therapy. You implied that otherwise therapy would be a waste of time.

The patient noted that the short hair made me seem an authoritarian. Being behind the desk I seemed like a king. In childhood he had fantasized about an authoritarian king, Richard III, defecating on him. The dream image and the childhood fantasy are both related to his view of his father as a man who frequently and apparently arbitrarily explodes in rage at him. As this example demonstrates, king and father can be easily connected.

Grey birds possess the speaker's heart in "Mary's Song," and again these birds could be considered phallic symbols of masculinity and, possibly, of the father also. Gutheil (1951) relates a frigid woman's dream of frustrating sexual intercourse:

> I am dead, but I feel and hear everything. I hear the wonderful song of a bird but not clearly enough. I concentrate all my senses in order to perceive it better. The tone seems to come nearer and nearer, and within the next moment I expect to hear it fully. But the tension will not relax. I cannot move, as I am dead. I can only hear the bird coming closer and then going farther away again. I feel extremely sad. (p. 376)

Here, birds are seen to be masculine. Plath's "grey birds" may be interpreted as masculine and possibly representative of the father. It should not be considered insignificant when Plath, in those poems more explicitly about the father, associates him with grey. In "Man in Black," part of his surroundings is the "grey sea." In "Daddy" he is described as a "statue with one grey toe," again a possible masculine phallic symbol. Just as black, death, and father are linked and used throughout the poetry, so are grey, death, and father; both the black father and the grey father obsess the speakers of the poems.

Related to blackness and greyness, shadows and shadowy objects that give an ominous and terrifying note are employed symbolically also. In "Candles" shadows stoop over a sleeping infant. The speaker is threatened by a devouring "shadow of doorways" in "Who." Seeming to be only tenuously connected to blackness and greyness, the shadow is perhaps not so strongly indicative of death as they are. Plath may possibly be basing her image on the shadow of death in the Psalms. How the shadow is connected to the father is perhaps even more difficult to understand; dream symbolism again may help here. The "shadow" can be that part of a person which he wants to reject, the "devil" as Gutheil (1951) calls it. In Plath's poetry it has already been seen that the personas of the poems recognize a black part of the mind, the black yew tree and the grey birds, and that this part seems to be connected to the father. In "Daddy" this motif is more explicit; the speaker wants to purge her mind of the father as a black devil and to reject the image of the father. From this psychological angle, a "shadow," as part of herself Plath wants to eliminate, could be connected with the father. Regarded somewhat differently, the father is reborn in the child, and this resurrection can be symbolized by the shadow. The images in the poems, nevertheless, only barely connect the shadow to the father. For instance, in "Ouija" the Ouija board, which hymns of death, is personified as a masculine, cold, black god of shades. The images of the colossus in "The Colossus" serve to make the connection more evident. The speaker is literally attempting to put together a statue, explicitly referred to as her father. Figuratively, she is attempting to unify her mental conception of him, put him in perspective, to sort out, understand, and reconcile her feelings toward him. For thirty years she has struggled with her conception of her father, and she images her life as being intimately tied up with his. "My hours are married to a shadow." She cannot eliminate her father from her mind and from her life; he shadows her.

Ice, snow, and frost (frozen water) and their coldness represent death in almost all their appearances. The speaker in "Frog Autumn" portrays the coming of autumn as the arrival of death and notes that "frost drops even the spider." If in "Tulips" the speaker at the beginning of the poem is nonchalant in mentioning that she is "snowed-in," by the end of the poem one realizes that the snow foreshadows the idea that she is oppressed by imminent death.

Since to be dead is to be cold, coldness easily relates to death. Another of my patients, a young woman, dreamt of an old, gnarled woman who was like ice. The patient associated the old woman with her emotionally dead mother, and to be like her mother was to be dead. For Plath, coldness just as easily can be related to the father.

Throughout *The Colossus* the father's surroundings are cold. In "Full Fathom Five" he lives in the cold sea and floats near ice mountains, and in "Man in Black" he walks over March ice. The cold father haunts the speakers of the poems for, as "A Winter Ship" puts it, the sea is "an albatross of frost." Here again the important image (ice) is connected to both death and a masculine phallic symbol, the albatross, the bird. The association of the father and coldness probably indicates his emotional coldness. The river's calling is described as "ice-hearted" in "Lorelei." Just as the personas incorporate the deathly, black, evil father and make part of their minds black, they incorporate the father's deadly coldness and become figuratively dead. In "Spinster" the widow longs for the "heart's frosty discipline"; in "The Moon and the Yew Tree" the mind is cold; in "Wintering" the body is cold; and in "Last Words" the speaker's feet, still another symbolic reference to the male sexual organ, grow cold.

Possibly because of its inanimacy or because of its use as a headstone on a grave, the stone or rock is also employed to symbolize death. Though its symbolic use seems to be unusual, like the sea, it is one of Plath's major images and is used in conjunction with many of the others discussed. Part of the annihilating landscape of "Hardcastle Crags" is the "black stone set/On black stone." These stones particularly threaten death:

> but before the weight
> Of stones and hills of stones could break
> Her down to mere quartzy grit in that stony light
> She turned back.

In a comparable use of the image, the ominous godmothers in "The Disquieting Muses" threaten death as they "stand their vigil in gowns of stone." From another angle, a man dying is seen as turning to stone, so when the threat of death is fulfilled, the victim becomes stone dead. In "All the Dead Dears," the female skeleton lies with a "granite grin." Speaker after speaker in the poems images himself as a stone and, hence, dead. In "The Stones" the speaker becomes a "still pebble"; in "Parliament Hill Fields" the speaker concludes "I'm stone"; and in "Who" the same impulse is evident, "I am a root, a stone. . . ." When dead, one is stone. This last approach suggests and results in a minor but related death image. The human body is viewed as a statue or a piece of sculpture. In "The Surgeon at 2 A.M." the patient is thought of as a Roman statue, his inner organs as "stones/To rattle in a bottle." In "Finisterre" the Lady of the Shipwrecked has marble skirts and is the object of prayer by a marble sailor. As erections memorializing the dead, statues appropriately are associated with death.

Inevitably, the father is associated with all these images of stone, rocks, and sculpture. He is portrayed striding across stones in "Man in Black." In "The Beekeeper's Daughter," the father's foot (a phallic symbol) which is stepping on the daughter's heart, is called the "sister of a stone." Spreading throughout his whole body, his emotional hardness makes him entirely rigid; he is seen as a massive piece of sculpture in "The Colossus" and as a marble-heavy ghastly statue in "Daddy." Emotional hardness is not the only element which makes the statue an appropriate image of the father. Statues can represent the male phallus in dreams, and there is an apposition based on unconscious symbolization.

> Let us now shed some light upon the significance of *monuments*. As memorial structures, monuments, as a rule, represent memories. Their oblong shape (obelisk) may in some dreams be the reason for their being used as sexual (phallic) symbols. *Totem poles* and *tombstones* are known to have such significance. Also the use in dreams of monuments in association with the cemetery and death is plausible. (Gutheil, 1951, p. 140)

Haunted by this stony, male figure, it is natural for Plath to write a poem on the Medusa who turns humans to stone, just as the imaged father or male figure did in "The Rival." The male's "first gift is making stone out of everything," so that numerous personas become stone. In "Elm" there is a threat to make the head a stone, and in "Paralytic" the mind becomes a rock. Just as the daughter can become black and cold in response to the deadly father, the wife can become a perfectly carved diamondlike slave in "On Deck." The writer can identify completely with death and the father: "I become a still pebble" ("The Stones"). It can be seen now why the rocky scenes in "Hardcastle Crags" and "Wuthering Heights" are ominous, how rocks can have grudges in "Finisterre." The hard, phallic father hides behind those rocks.

Since in "Totem" the speaker is appalled by a cobra and in "Ouija" the queen of death has "wormy couriers," the serpent or snake seems to represent death. The appropriateness of this image seems to lie in the simple facts that graves contain worms and that snakes can kill. The latter aspect is developed in "Medallion" in which the bronze snake is described as "knifelike. . . . Pure death's metal." Interpreting the snake symbolically clarifies obscure lines in poems such as "Suicide Off Egg Rock" where it is noted that the words in the victim's book "wormed off the pages" leaving blank paper. This image seems to indicate the imminent suicide of the man who, like the marshals and admirals in "The Swarm," will worm his way into a mausoleum or to death. Imaged as a devil in

"Daddy," the father is clearly linked to the serpent by his evilness. Dream symbolism can show a deeper appropriateness of this association. Freud (1900) considers the snake one of the most important unconscious symbols of the male sexual organ. Gutheil (1951) explores this connection throughout history and myth:

> The snake worshippers attributed to the snake divine powers, but the connection between phallic concepts and serpent worship in many epochs of human history is unmistakable. It is particularly the *paternal* phallus which finds its symbolization in the serpent cult. In the disguise of a snake, Apollo seduces Atys, Zeus seduces Persephone, and Odin seduces Gunnlodh. Snakes were held sacred in the temple of Aesculapius, son of Apollo, where they represented the god himself. (p. 136)

It is not at all unusual to link the father with the snake. In "Elm" the speaker is terrified by murderous faces whose snaky, acidic kisses kill; the linkage of the father, the serpent, and death seems to suggest that it is the father's face which terrorizes the speaker. Just as Plath writes poems controlled by her other images of the deadly father, grey in "The Thin People," black in "Man in Black," stones in "The Stones," she writes a poem on snakes, "Snakecharmer." The snakecharmer creates a world of snakes, a world of nothing but snakes. Though a humorous poem, if read symbolically, it is also an ominous one for Plath has already linked the snake with the knife, another male sex symbol, in "Medallion."

Perhaps the strangest image of death is the machine. In "Night Shift" the speaker, hearing construction men at work, realizes that the "greased machines" stun the marrow. The most pervasive mechanical image is that of a railroad locomotive or engine. In "Tulips" the tulips, which by the end of the poem symbolize death, are compared to a "rust-red engine." In "Getting There" the speaker images a train as the black car of Lethe with teeth like the devil's. The black wheels that are apparently carrying her to her death, like the cobra, appall her. In "Totem" the locomotive kills the track, while in "Stings" the self sought by the speaker has been killed by an engine. We see that even these specific, descriptive details of the modern age can be understood as symbols that convey Plath's thematic concerns. The prospective victim is in a landscape of gas tanks and factory stacks in "Suicide Off Egg Rock." These elements not only create an atmosphere of starkness and desolation, but they also connote or covertly symbolize the coming suicide. Gas can be associated with carbon monoxide, one means of suicide; factories are abstracted machinery. Later in the poem, the suicide's body is imaged as a machine, and this image then signifies his death. If it is strange that the image of the machine is used to symbolize death, it perhaps is more unusual that the machine is connected with the father. The rationale for these connections seems to lie in Plath's image of the father as a German Nazi in "Daddy." The father, as a Nazi, is responsible for the death train which conveys the speaker to the concentration camp. Following up this association, the speaker then images him as a tank, "panzer-man, panzer-man." In a related poem, "Man in Black," the father is again made mechanical: "riveting stones, air,/All of it, together." Looked at psychoanalytically, the joining of the father, the machine, and death, especially in the locomotive, is not surprising. On the one hand, the locomotive could be a male sex symbol. "It is highly probable that all complicated machinery and apparatus occurring in dreams stand for the genitals (and as a rule male ones)" (Freud, 1900, p. 356). On the other hand, departure by train can be a symbol of death (Freud, 1900). Knowing that the father and the machine are linked helps explain why in "Getting There" the German train is black and has wheels like the devil's teeth, why in "Stings" the inner self being sought has been killed by an engine, and why in "Suicide Off Egg Rock" factory stacks loom in the background of the suicide. "Years," a poem which uses numerous images of death (darkness, freezing, and blackness), probably expresses an ambivalent response toward the father:

> What I love is
> The piston in motion —
> My soul dies before it.

The machine is loved, but is deadly anyway. At the end of the poem, the piston is further linked with the father as serpent: "In blue distance the pistons hiss."

Plath's personas mirror her view of the father. Just as the father is seen as blackness, a stone, coldness, and a snake, the speakers identify themselves similarly. Minds are black and cold, while people become stones and snakes. On the one hand, the identification of these images can be explained as symbols of death. Since the dead father is a stone, any dead or figuratively dead person can be described as a stone. On the other hand, Plath presents another possible reason. In "Daddy" the speaker, though extremely hostile, states that through dying she wants to get back to, not back at, her father. By becoming a stone, a rock, or a snake, the personas reach the father, identify with him, or incorporate him. They reach the father by becoming him in death.

All these images work both singly and together. Usually in poem after poem and in volume after volume they are employed in groups. Each image becomes just a part of a vast complex of images all working toward the same end, to image death. In *The Colossus*, in "Hardcastle Crags," where the speaker seems to be on the verge of being annihilated by the crags, the landscape has steely streets, iron hills, black stones, shadowy crags, and the sea. In *Ariel's* "Tulips," a poem expressing a sense of encroaching death, the tulips are imagined to be stones and engines, and the speaker, snowed-in by the environment and by drinking water, sees herself as a pebble, a shadow, and water. *Crossing the Water* (Plath, 1971) contains more poems with this set of images than the other two volumes. "Parliament Hill Fields" employs stone, snow, water, cloud (another symbol of death), and shadow. "A Life" uses sea, shadow, grey, cloud, and cold. The fact that these images appear in all three volumes of the poetry supports Lucie-Smith's (1966) suggestion that there is no dramatic break between *The Colossus* and *Ariel*; rather, there is a continual concern with the same themes which are conveyed by the same or similar images.

Otherwise obscure poems become clear through a symbolic reading in terms of this complex structure of images of death and of the father. For example, "Totem" of *Ariel*, though seeming to call for an interpretation of the father, is at first unclear because of the apparent lack of a concept to unify its diverse images. A totem, of course, is a substitute for the father, and what might be expected in this poem is the annual ritual feast of eating the totem animal. According to Freud's (1913b) speculation, sons, children, or tribal brothers can express in the totemic system and its taboos their ambivalent feelings toward the father. During most of the year the eating of the totem animal, the father-substitute, is prohibited and persons under this injunction honor the father. By feasting on the animal once a year, the person can indulge his murderous feelings. Plath inverts the ritual of the annual feast. It is not the father-substitute who is eaten, it is, rather, the child-substitute. In the poetry of Plath, the deadly father always wins.

The speaker's images of death in "Totem" show the father as victor. The first image presents a train engine, travelling at night and surrounded by drowned fields. The engine is killing and eating its silver track. The presence of the black night, watery fields, and a locomotive seems to indicate the parallel presence of the father. The father is killing innocence or purity, symbolized by silver. The second image seems to present farmers as pigs being conveyed by trains to the slaughter-house. This image is reminiscent of the Nazi trains and concentration camps in other poems. What is interesting here is that the pigs do not seem to represent the father but rather the child. The murder weapons, cleavers and guillotines, are masculine symbols that Plath has previously associated with the father and death. The victim, called a baby and Christ, is apparently human and innocent. Just as the first two images of death, the locomotive and the cutting blades, are masculine, so is the third. Shifting to the first person, the speaker questions whether the cobra and its "eye of the mountains" shall appall her. It seems again that the father as serpent and rock is the underlying threat. The last image of death is a new one: a spider devours some flies. Though the spider as a dream symbol has no fixed meaning, it can be associated at times with a masculine figure. Given the context, Plath herself provides enough clues. Though the reader cannot explicitly identify the spider with the father, the speaker of the poem images the flies as "blue children," and these children are roped in by infinite death. It seems then that the totemic ritual has been inverted. It is the father in the images of the train, the night, the drowned fields, the cleavers, the cobra, the mountains, and the spider, who eats the innocent child, imaged as the track, the baby pigs, and the flies. In "Totem," as in many other poems, the speaker cannot escape the multitudinous images of the father. These images are aptly summed up in the last lines of "Totem." In Sylvia Plath's poems, the father is "the one/Death with its many sticks."

# Form and Content:
# Dom Moraes's Poetry

With its particular stress on seeing the literary text as an organic whole, twentieth-century literary criticism demands that the style or the formal elements of the text be examined as an integrated part of that whole.

> If we are to emphasize, not the special subject matter, but the way in which the poem is built, or — to change the metaphor — the form which it has taken as it *grew* in the poet's mind, we shall necessarily raise questions of formal structure and rhetorical organization: we shall be forced to talk about levels of meanings, symbolizations, clashes of connotations, paradoxes, ironies, etc.
>
> Moreover, however inadequate these terms may be, even so, such terms do bring us closer, I feel, to the structure of the poem as an organism. (Brooks, 1947, p. 218)

Though this approach has its advantages, the view which usually accompanies it — that reference to knowledge outside the text, like anthropological or psychoanalytic knowledge, distracts us from it — is too limiting. Use of such knowledge can give us an increased awareness of the relation and integration of the form and content of a literary work. In so doing, it brings us closer to the work itself.

In the case of a foreign poet writing in English, an understanding of his cultural background can be especially helpful in guiding us to the important elements of his artistic style. In examining the poetry of Indian poet Dom Moraes in this context, I shall (1) elucidate the two distinct poetic and cultural traditions that have influenced him; (2) explore the Indian culture he grew up in; and (3) explicate two poems with the Indian influences especially in mind.

The Indian poet Dom Moraes has been influenced by both Eastern and Western cultures since his birth in Bombay in 1938. Born into an India still under the rule of the British, he had continued contacts with the West even after the British left. He travelled abroad with his father, who was fulfilling journalistic assignments, and went to England at sixteen to attend Oxford University. Moraes has spent most of his adult life in England. His commitment to the West is now and again evidenced by frequent residences there.

This Western influence extends to his poetry. Poets such as T. S. Eliot, W. H. Auden, and Stephen Spender are acknowledged mentors. Spender, after meeting Moraes in India, encouraged and sponsored the young poet. W. B. Yeats and Dylan Thomas also seem to have been of some significance in his development. Eliot's imagery of the modern wasteland and his religious concerns are particularly evident in Moraes' earliest volume, *A Beginning* (1957), in which images of resurrection and especially stones predominate: "on every tree we see the sign/Of the black frost that cracks the stony year" ("Words to a Dancer"). Thomas's work seems close to Moraes's "A Man Dreaming." Yeats's trimeter shows up in Moraes's later work in *Poems* (1960), *John Nobody* (1965), and *Poems 1955–1965* (1965), *e.g.*, "Craxton," "The Children" and "Prophet." The poet's apocalytic visions and cyclical view of history, appearing in "Local History," may be Yeatsian. Furthermore, Moraes has sometimes been seen as influenced by the British "Movement" poets such as Philip Larkin, because of his wry tone.

In addition to apparent Western influences, Moraes's work has connections and similarities with that of other Indian poets writing in English, such as P. Lal, Nissim Ezekiel, Kamala Das, and H. D. Katrak, to name a few. Indian poetry in English has begun to take on characteristic qualities (Nandy, 1971), although these qualities seem to be derived from Western modernism. The 1959 Kavita Manifesto by P. Lal and K. Raghavendra Rao stated the goals Indian poetry in English should embrace. They emphasized that poetry should deal in concrete terms with concrete experience, that it should be precise and disciplined, and that it should be lyrical. These standards were formed partially in reaction to the earlier imitation of Western poetry by Indian writers. Moraes, at times, has been accused of being too romantic and too sentimental, but to a large degree he does follow the standards set by Lal and Rao. For instance, "Craxton" is tightly structured and well focused with precise imagery, "A snail oils the sill." Amalendu Bose (1968) has recently examined the characteristic qualities of Indian poetry in English further and points to its consciousness of the verbal medium, evidenced by words themselves as the subject of poems. Moraes illustrates this interest in the medium in his own individual way. A look at his titles discloses his consciousness of the verbal form of the poem: "Words to a Dancer," "Words to a Boy," "Verses for Peter Levi, S. J.," "Hawk Song," "Song about the Usual Subject," "A Letter," "Letter to my Mother," and "Speech in the Desert." Even more prevalent is Moraes' concern with the function of poetry, his role as a poet, and the relation of his poetry to his life. He faces these questions in his early work. In "Autobiography" (1965) he says:

> I have grown up, hand on the primal bone,
> Making the poem, taking the word from the stream,
> Fighting the sand for speech, fighting the stone.

He faces these questions in his later poems, as in "Craxton"

(1965a), "My humped hand idles." Moraes follows both a Western line of poetic development and a more locally Indian line of development. The similarity of contemporary Indian poetry in English, with its emphasis on concreteness and the verbal medium, to the Western modernist, new critical movement, with its concern with precise imagery and verbal structures, is apparent. Here too Moraes's style is in essence Western.

As a poet concerned with facing the problems of solitude and death and with seeking new values to live by (Mollinger, 1974), Moraes is also in the modern Western tradition, but in his poetic handling of these subjects and of other personal concerns, he is not totally Western. In defining the poet's particular and individual poetic voice and style, after having noted the influence of Western poets and styles, one must take special care to acknowledge the "easternness" of the poetry. It is easy for Westerners to think of Moraes as a confessional poet. Just as Robert Lowell writes of his mental hell in "Man and Wife" and "Skunk Hour," Moraes writes of his own emotional emptiness in "John Nobody." Just as Sylvia Plath is obsessed with death, especially her own, throughout her poetry, Moraes has the same morbid concerns from the time of his early "Moz" and "Words to a Dancer" to his later "Homo Sapiens" (1965a), "Announce my death in words of one syllable." Sexual experiences or fantasies, including possible homosexual ones ("Vivasection"), also appear in the poetry. Though it seems clear that Moraes is a poet who writes of intensely personal subjects, it is well to remember that he was born in India and was necessarily influenced by Eastern thought, whatever his personal religion. What from a Western viewpoint seems "confessional," might from an Eastern perspective seem otherwise.

C. G. Jung's differentiation of Eastern and Western thinking, though by no means definitive, may be helpful in pointing to the meanings of particular aspects of Moraes's poetry. Jung (1939) calls attention to a chief difference between the East and the West: "Introversion is, if one may so express it, the 'style' of the East, a habitual and collective attitude, just as extraversion is the 'style' of the West" (p. 481). Simply put, the introvert is mainly concerned with his inner life; however, Jung points out the complexities which result from introversion. The introverted attitude by isolating the subjective factor, "calls forth the characteristic manifestations of the unconscious . . . the sense of indefiniteness, timelessness, oneness" (p. 491). The introvert is in close touch with the unconscious and hence, in Freud's terminology, with primary process thinking. Focus on objects is indefinite; objects and ideas can be condensed into one; they merge. Boundaries between objects and the self are not firm permitting the self and the object to be viewed as one. As Jung puts it, for the Eastern mind the psyche is all-important: "All existence emanates from it, and all separate forms dissolve back into it" (p. 482).

Recent psychoanalytic thought has reached similar conclusions. Observing the Indian scene, Erikson (1969) finds one word which unites all his perceptions, fusion: "Indians want to give and to get by fusing — actively and passively" (pp. 40–41). The self-abandonment of the Kama Sutra and of the erotic sculptures of Khajarao are *immersions* in sexual license, and the dependent longing for the "family" (including aunts, uncles, and cousins) is a search for a fusion which affirms the self. Such a search relates to the remnants of an early developmental stage in which the distinction between the self and the other has not become clear:

> The initial blurring between mother and child from which the sense of self begins to evolve. In the beginning there is always oneness — a coalescence of child with all that is, unbounded as to time, space, and sense of self. (Rose, 1972, p. 181)

Kakar (1978) has recently traced the influence of this stage on Indian personality and thought.

It is this "oneness" between subject and object which is important to understanding Dom Moraes's poetic technique and, consequently, the meanings of his poems. In many of his poems, subjects, images, and symbols are reflections or projections of his own self. From a Jungian perspective, his psyche has transformed "material objects into psychic images," a typically Eastern mode. From a more contemporary psychoanalytic perspective, there exists a fluidity between psyche and external world in which internal images of the self and the world are unified and merged. Appropriately enough, this technique appears with especial clarity in two poems concerned with the East: "Kanheri Caves" (Moraes, 1957) and "Letter to my Mother" (Moraes, 1965a).

"Kanheri Caves" refers to the second-century A. D. Buddhist Caves outside Bombay. It is structured and organized on a principle of oneness. The images of material objects are the psychic images of the speaker. There are three major image clusters: the Kanheri Caves and the surrounding Indian landscape, the mother, and the hawks and the British. All become reflections of the speaker's self which, in the end, show his emotional development.

The speaker's attitude toward the Buddhist caves and India mirrors his own depressed feelings. The Indian landscape is described as "blunted," "tormented," and "ambiguous." After the British leave India, the caves are "wrecked" by storms, the floors "crack," the stone blocks are "fallen," the statues of Buddha are awaiting their own "crash," and the atmosphere is full of "clouds." This negative description of India merges with a description of the speaker himself:

> this cliff
> Was colonized by a mild antique race,
> Who left us, . . .

Referring to the British withdrawal from India, the speaker identifies with India by the "us." This merger is hinted at earlier in the poem. "It seems this green ambiguous landscape tilts/And teeters the perspective of the eye." The ambiguous or distorted scene shifts to an uncertain perspective of the "eye" (or even "I").

When the speaker concentrates more specifically on a tomb in the cave, not only does this unity between India represented by Kanheri and the speaker become more clear, but

India, the cave, and the self merge with an image of the mother as well:

> a lonely tomb.
> I touch its side. The stone's worn smooth as flesh.
> A stranger dangles peaceful in that womb.
>
> Worm he will be, if born: blink in the sun.
> I'll crawl into his dark: perhaps he'll climb
> Beyond. . . .

The merger begins when the speaker touches the tomb; the material object, the tomb, becomes human — "flesh." In fact, it becomes the mother — "womb." (Unifying all these images, and on an unconscious level reinforcing their merger, is the fact that in the unconscious a country, cave, and tomb can all symbolize the mother.) At first, a "stranger" is in the womb-tomb, but then the speaker merges with the stranger. The "he" becomes "I'll," then becomes "he'll" again. There is no real differentiation between "he" and "I" here. Almost all has become one: India equals the speaker, the Indian tomb in the caves equals human flesh which equals the mother's womb, and the speaker equals the stranger within the womb-tomb of mother-India.

One further image remains: hawks. Flying above the caves, they come and go just as the British did. The possible oneness of the hawks, the British, and the speaker emerges in the final lines of the poem:

> Hawks in a hot concentric ecstasy
> Of flight and shriek will wake his vision. And,
> When the clouds lift, he'll glimpse the miles-off sea.

The hawks wake the "he," and the "he" now can see into the distance, even as the hawks high above can. The hawks merge with the "he" who previously was equated to the speaker. What the hawk-he-speaker glimpses may be Britain, far across the sea. In describing the play of Indian children, Erikson (1969) says there is "little differentiation between out-doors and indoors, jungle and city, or, indeed, one scene from

another" (p. 40). Moraes similarly fuses his images of the
countryside, other people, and himself.

In "Kanheri Caves" then, Moraes uses his images of material objects to reflect his psyche and emotions. Tormented
India and the "wrecked" caves mirror his self as it is. The
hawks and the British who come and go from India picture a
potential self. These "mergers" lead us to a thematic understanding of the poem. It is a poem of rebirth. The speaker, at
first tormented but at one with India, becomes one with the
stranger in the mother's womb-tomb. He emerges reborn as a
hawk looking toward Britain. This transition from the womb
to Britain is facilitated technically by the stranger being described as "peaceful" in the womb and the British, the
speaker's new identity, as "mild." There is a series of progressive identities which move the speaker from torment to vision
and from India to Britain. From that merger comes an individual: "Little by little the idea that Mother is distinct from
oneself begins to take shape and with it the idea of a self and
one's separateness in the world" (Rose, 1972, p. 181). Appropriately, the speaker in the poem seeks an identity in the West,
the land of individuals. As we shall see, again it is an identity
through fusion.

A brief examination of "Letter to my Mother" shows how
Moraes projects himself into India, his mother, and, again in
a minor way, Britain. The opening of the second section of the
poem indicates this clearly:

> Your eyes are like mine.
> When I last looked in them
> I saw my whole country,
> A defeated dream. . . .

Looking into his mother's eyes, he sees India. India's defeated
dream, exemplified in the poem by the "filthy sea," the hopeless "weepers in the bazaar," the "corroding sun," the "burnt"
Hindu corpses, and Bombay's sun-cooked Parsi corpses wait-
ing for the vultures, is mirrored by his mother's dream. As
noted later in the poem, "Your dream is desolate." The
speaker's merger with the mother, "Your eyes are like mine,"

is further emphasized by an observation on shame: "I was ashamed of myself/Since I was ashamed of you." In one sense, the "you" is a mere stand-in grammatically and semantically for "myself." Just as in "Kanheri Caves" where the speaker's oneness with India and the mother is transient and partakes of the past, here in "Letter to my Mother" he emphasizes a new identity, a oneness with Britain. The poetic device of merging the object and the self in his imagery makes this clear, "I am tidying my life/In this cold, tidy country." England is tidy, the speaker is tidy; they are one. At the end of the poem he tells his mother he will not return to her, to India, or to his former desolate dream. "You know I will not return." Here we see the relevance of Erikson's point that Indians continually seek fusion: the speaker leaves a merger with India for a different merger, one with Britain.

Moraes, then, is more than a confessional poet in the contemporary tradition. He does write about extremely personal concerns, but he does so in a way that differentiates him from other contemporary poets. His style is distinct and integrated with the thematic concerns of his poems. Projecting and merging his own psyche with the material objects he deals with, he is similar to Walt Whitman, another poet who in writing about himself was also influenced by Eastern culture. As in "Song of Myself" Whitman, absorbing all to himself, can say, "of every hue and caste am I," so Moraes in these songs of himself merges with his past India and his future Britain, his Eastern past and his Western future.

# 8/THE LITERARY OEUVRE

# Levels of Meaning: Wallace Stevens's Poetry

Psychoanalytic critics have shown that works of literature have psychological meanings concomitant with their more traditional aesthetic, literary, and intellectual meanings. For example, I have argued, in Chapter 5, that Herman Melville's "Bartleby the Scrivener: A Story of Wall Street" is, in one sense, about the desire to be fed and taken care of. In Chapter 6, I pointed out that Sylvia Plath's poetry has clusters of father images. In Chapter 3, I showed how Wallace Stevens's poetry uses the archetypal hero. In this chapter, I shall argue that intellectual/philosophical and emotional/psychological meanings are integrally connected in the poetic oeuvre of Wallace Stevens.

Interest in the poetry of Wallace Stevens continues to grow at an extraordinary rate. There are now over thirty book-length studies and innumerable critical articles that appear year after year. Despite the continued appearance of publications, the general thematic limits of Stevens's work has been set for some time. Stevens is concerned with the nature of reality; he wonders whether it is composed only of the external, physical world. He questions whether man can live in a purely natural world—by bread alone and without God. Stevens is concerned with the imagination; he questions whether the mind creates all that man sees, whether man lives in a purely mental world. Hesitatingly believing in philosophic idealism at times, he wonders whether belief in the imagination and poetry can serve as a substitute for a belief in God. Can the imagination provide human values and ordering principles in an apparently chaotic world? Throughout his poetry Stevens attempts to choose between a belief that the physical world is the only reality and a belief in the ideal creations of the imagination. But he is a doubter. He doubts his own positions repeatedly. From a belief in naturalism to a belief in idealism, from a belief in the value of poetry to a belief in its inadequacy, Wallace Stevens continually vacillates.

This brief summary does not do the poetry justice, of course, but it does suggest that Stevens is a meditative poet interested in ideas and philosophical questions. At times, his poems are extremely vague. They are abstract, general, and perhaps too intellectual. His symbols might be considered obscure and unfamiliar. Some critics, such as Randall Jarrell, feel that there is an absence of human passion and emotion in the poetry. Stevens (1957) himself seems to note the lack of emotion in his poetry and in his life: "Life is an affair of people not of places. But for me life is an affair of places and that is the trouble" (p. 158). Given the great interest in this poet's works, one wonders whether there is more than dry, abstract intellectualizations and philosophical meditations in the poetry. There may be elements in the poetry which have strong emotional attraction and coloration. In a comment on "The Emperor of Ice-Cream" in *The Explicator* (1948), Stevens suggests the importance of the poem's emotional meanings.

Things that have their origin in the imagination or in the emotions (poems) very often have meanings that differ in nature from the meanings of things that have their origin in reason. They have imaginative or emotional meanings, not rational meanings, and they communicate these meanings to people who are susceptible to imaginative or emotional meanings. They may communicate nothing at all to people who are open only to rational meanings. In short, things that have their origin in the imagination or in the emotions very often take on a form that is ambiguous or uncertain. It is not possible to attach a single, rational meaning to such things without destroying the imaginative or emotional ambiguity or uncertainty that is inherent in them and that is why poets do not like to explain. That the meanings given by others are sometimes meanings not intended by the poet or that were never present in his mind does not impair them as meanings.

The poems do have intellectual meanings, or as Stevens says, rational ones. They also have emotional meanings which accompany their evident intellectual ones. At the same time that they are satisfying conscious, intellectual interests, they are also satisfying unconscious desires with strong emotional elements. As Holland (1968) puts it, "But all stories — and all literature — have this basic way of meaning: they transform the unconscious fantasy discoverable through psychoanalysis into the conscious meanings discovered by conventional interpretation" (p. 28). Holland implies that literature has not only unconscious meanings but in addition that literature has conscious and unconscious meanings integrally connected to one another. In this essay I shall examine one of Stevens's basic themes, his commitment to naturalism and to the natural world, and its emotional underpinnings — oedipal fantasies and desires. I will attempt to show (1) that poems portraying a commitment to the natural world also portray the sexual act; (2) that the natural earth is imaged as the mother, and, thus, the poet's commitment to the earth is a sexual approach to the mother as well; and (3) that the expected oedipal concomitant, rivalry with the father, also appears in the poetry.

"Ploughing on Sunday" is usually interpreted from a rational perspective either as portraying the poet creating the myths of his country or as picturing man's dedication to the natural world (Sukenick, 1967). In the context of Stevens's typical themes, this poem shows his naturalistic impulse. In a more complex way, it shows his desire to have imagination, poetry, based on reality, the earth. The imagery and mood of the poem indicate clearly that this poem is, however, a revelry in phallic pride and in an orgy of coitus and ejaculation:

> The white cock's tail
> Tosses in the wind
> The turkey-cock's tail
> Glitters in the sun.
>
> Water in the fields.
> The wind pours down.
> The feathers flare
> And bluster in the wind.
>
> Remus, blow your horn!
> I'm ploughing on Sunday,
> Ploughing North America.
> Blow your horn!
>
> Tum-ti-tum,
> Ti-tum-tum-tum!
> The turkey-cock's tail
> Spreads to the sun.
>
> The white cock's tail
> Streams to the moon.
> Water in the fields.
> The wind pours down.

Just as sexual symbols and puns appear throughout Stevens's poetry in general, phallic symbols abound throughout this poem: "cock," "tail," "feathers," and "horn." Not only are birds and cocks traditionally viewed as phallic symbols, but the words themselves are used colloquially to refer to the phallus. In the poem these phalluses are proud, boastful, and energetically active—tossing, glittering, flaring, blustering, and spreading—and all of them seem to be pointing upward. The use of active verbs in describing the white cock and the turkey-cock is appropriate, for they lead to the climax of the

poem: "Water in the fields./The wind pours down." Both
these images are ejaculatory. In literature, the wind traditionally stands for creativity. In mythology and in alchemy, it
more specifically represents the power of fecundity. Here, it is
pouring down like rain, a liquid, or semen. In the image of the
water in the fields, the water, as a liquid, also is semen-like.
The fields, as part of the earth, stand for femininity. The
fields relate to the major image of the poem, the ploughing.
The speaker, Remus' brother Romulus, who ploughed a furrow to describe the boundaries of Rome when he founded it
and the Roman race, is "ploughing North America." On one
level he is creating a poetic image of it; on another, he is
making love to the earth, after the manner of Whitman:
"Smile O voluptuous cool-breath'd earth! . . . Smile, for
your lover comes." Just as Whitman makes use of two meanings of "comes," Stevens makes use of the double meaning of
"ploughing." Ploughing is preparatory to seeding or fertiliz-
ing. In Hindu mythology, Sita is born from a field furrow.
The earth, accordingly, is traditionally seen as feminine. The
image of a farmer ploughing is symbolic of the speaker making love.

The poem can be interpreted from several perspectives,
and the sexual one supports the others. First, the poem expresses Stevens' basic theme: man's commitment to the natural world. The sexual meaning supports this intellectual one;
the speaker shows his complete commitment to the earth by
making love to it. Secondly, the poem is about the creative
poet and his relation to the earth. The agricultural imagery of
fertilization, the image of the wind as creative spirit, the birds
as symbols of the imagination, and the allusion to the birth of
Rome are all appropriate to this theme. The physical creativity of the sexual act supports the theme of imaginative creativity. Finally, the poem presents an act to which we all can
respond emotionally. All the images are sexual ones: the
speaker as farmer ploughs the feminine earth and, as Romulus, gives birth to a city. Phallic symbols move energetically

upward until images of emission take over. The sexual imagery should not be viewed as merely supporting the intellectual meanings. The poem should be seen as controlled by, and organized around an image or a fantasy of the sexual act. From this fantasy the poem gets its emotional impact. As Stevens (1957) says, "A poet looks at the world as a man looks at a woman" (p. 165).

This connection between Stevens's naturalistic theme and a coital fantasy appears throughout the poetry, sometimes clearly, sometimes in more obscure forms. For instance, in "Hymn from a Watermelon Pavilion," a particularly difficult poem, the symbolism still is transparent, and the sexual fantasy shows through. The few critics who attempt to explain this poem do so by typing it with "Ploughing on Sunday," to show a choice of the natural, real world over an imaginary one (Sukenick, 1967). This poem is similar to "Ploughing on Sunday" not only in its intellectual meaning but also in the sexual fantasy it embodies. The speaker in this poem is just what he is called — a lover. In choosing the earthly world, the speaker chooses a real watermelon over an imaginary purple one. Fruit has been considered feminine throughout history, and a watermelon, with its oval hollow containing water and seeds, might particularly be considered a symbol of the feminine sexual organ. The fruit can be considered the equivalent to the egg and a symbol of earthly desires. The symbolization of the lover and the watermelon is clarified by the expected sexual embrace of the earthly:

> A feme may come, leaf-green,
> Whose coming may give revel
> Beyond revelries of sleep,
> Yes, and the blackbird spread its tail. . . .

A green woman comes (perhaps sexually also) to bring delight, and in expectation a bird lifts its phallic tail. The phallic symbolism of the blackbird is supported by previous images that are meant to tempt the lover to commit himself to the earthly: "Here is the plantain by your door/And the best cock of red feather. . . ." The plantain, a bananalike plant, the ever present cock, and the feather all have phallic connotations. Tempted by the cock and the feme, is it any wonder that the lover ends on an exclamatory note: "Rise . . . And hail, cry hail, cry hail"? From this perspective, like "Ploughing on Sunday," "Hymn from a Watermelon Pavilion" expresses an embrace of the earthly, natural world. From another perspective, the poem embodies the desire for woman and sex. The image of the earth as a woman is used as before, but here the use of the image is clearer. In "Ploughing on Sunday" the realization of the sexual meaning was made difficult by the symbolization. Here, since the symbols are clearer, the sexual meaning of the poem is lost in the obscurities of the rest of the poem (for traditional, universal symbols, see Gutheil, 1951, and Cirlot, 1962).

The figure of the earth as woman and the figure of the lover as one who embraces the earth is sometimes more disguised and sometimes less in Stevens's work, but these figures appear throughout. "The Hand as a Being," usually interpreted as the self's encounter with natural reality, like "Ploughing on Sunday," seems to present a fantasy of an orgasmic experience. The remarkably quite similar lyric of "Notes Toward a Supreme Fiction" III, x, has a sexual component also. It uses the symbol of the phallic tree, first developed in "Le Monocle de Mon Oncle." Other poems which show the acceptance of nature as sexual intercourse are "Notes Toward a Supreme Fiction" II, viii, in which Nanzia Nunzio strips, and "An Ordinary Evening in New Haven" in which the Ruler of Reality lies with the Queen of Fact. An examination of all these poems suggests that Stevens's images of his intellectual theme of earthly acceptance embody sexual, coital satisfactions. This is not to say that his acceptance of the earth is his main theme and that it only is imagined sexually. Rather, there are two levels to the one idea. The basic emotional theme is the sexual coition; the intellectual counterpart of this theme is the acceptance of the earthly. At times, the sexual impulses are not completely obscured and the sexual theme becomes nearly explicit. At other times, the sexual desires and themes are obscured by intellectualization, by abstraction, and by the technique of making the sexual theme into a mere metaphor for illustrating and deepening an intellectual idea.

Just as it is not unusual to personify the earth or nature as a woman, it is common to personify her as a mother. Here we shall begin to see the peculiarly oedipal trait of this basic Stevens' theme. Doggett (1966) extensively examined Stevens' archetype of the woman and pointed out her maternal characteristics; however, by concentrating on a Jungian analysis of the poetic images, he de-emphasized the sexual implications. These sexual implications are present and are connected with the mother as we have seen. As Holland (1966) says, "a work of literature builds on an oedipal fantasy whenever . . . it makes us feel fairly realistic versions of adult love" (p. 47). "Ploughing on Sunday" and "Hymn from a Watermelon Pavilion" do exactly that. They make us *feel*, not think about, adult sexual love. If commitment to the natural earth is sexual and if the earth is imaged as the mother, there may be an oedipal component to Stevens's theme. Since Doggett (1966) has extensively connected the earth to the mother, I shall examine the heretofore unnoted sexual elements just briefly. In addition to the metaphorical images of the earth as mother in "Anatomy of Monotony" and "Meditation Celestial & Terrestrial," there are explicit references to the mother as a possible lover. For instance, in "Le Monocle de Mon Oncle," a poem overtly about sex and love, the opening invocation is usually interpreted as addressed to the uncle's wife or lover: " 'Mother of heaven, regina of the clouds. . . .' " As Freud notes in *The Interpretation of Dreams*, the queen is used in dreams as a representation of the mother; the second epithet in the verse reinforces the maternal elements of the first. Though the speaker states that his invocation mocks the woman, it is not clear in what way. Is it done by idealizing her or making her virginal? Apparently she is quite sensual, for when he thinks of her he figuratively has an emission: "A deep up-pouring from some saltier well/Within me, bursts its watery syllable."

A poem which implies still more strongly that the mother is the sexual object is "Depression Before Spring." Like "Ploughing on Sunday," this poem embodies an emission fantasy; however, the mother who is the desired object does not appear:

> The cock crows
> But no queen rises.
>
> The hair of my blonde
> Is dazzling,
>
> As the spittle of cows
> Threading the wind.
>
> Ho! Ho!
>
> But ki-ki-ri-ki
> Brings no rou-cou.
>
> But no queen comes
> In slipper green.

The cock, as usual, implies the phallus; the queen, if Freud is right, implies the mother. There is the possible pun on "comes." The slipper hints of the bedroom. The ejaculation, apparently masturbatory, is imaged in the second stanza. When the cock crows, the ejaculation follows, imaged as a frothy liquid in the fecund wind. As in the sexual fantasies of the other poems, the climax is greeted triumphantly — "Ho! Ho!" — even though the mating calls — "ki-ki-ri-ki" — have failed to produce the real mother.

The sexual implications of this poem, and of the poems in general, have been ignored. Though the reader responds intuitively to them, he probably would rather not understand in conceptual terms their emotional meanings. Similar poems have been studied in great depth; but the obscured sexual desire for the mother has remained unnoticed.

The poem following "Depression Before Spring" in *The Collected Poems*, "The Emperor of Ice-Cream," has been much written about. The first stanza is usually interpreted as a revelry in sensual pleasure. The sexual nature of the images, particularly in the first few lines, has been observed (Thackaberry, 1948):

> Call the roller of big cigars,
> The muscular one, and bid him whip
> In kitchen cups concupiscent curds.

The difficulty in giving a comprehensive interpretation of the poem has always been the second stanza which apparently pictures a dead corpse. It has been noted earlier that Stevens recognizes the validity of seeking an emotional meaning to this poem. It is possible that the image of the woman in this second stanza is a highly repressed image of the mother. If so, it would then accompany, as in "Depression Before Spring," the masturbatory acts of the first stanza. The corpse seems to be of an older woman, necessarily made nonsexual. She is dead, "cold," and her feet are "horny." This interpretation might clarify the "fat girl" lyric of "Notes Toward a Supreme Fiction" III, x, in which the speaker, civilly hiding his (phallic) tree, addresses the fat girl of the earth. Calling the fat girl "madam," he apparently realizes that she is already someone's wife. He images her as child might see a mother: "when I think of you as strong or tired,/Bent over work, anxious, content, alone. . . ." This image gives the impression of being a screen-memory, to use a psychoanalytic term. It is a collage of memories recalled because of association with more important experiences or desires, possibly in this case, sexual desires toward the mother. The phallic symbolism of the tree of "Le Monocle de Mon Oncle" can be understood, with difficulty, because it shows desire for a wife. The phallic symbolism of the tree in the lyric of "Notes Toward a Supreme Fiction" is probably more obscure because it shows a desire for the tabooed mother.

"Ploughing on Sunday" and "Depression Before Spring" indicate that oedipal material operates in Stevens's poems. In addition to sexual desire for the mother, there is a somewhat obscured rivalry with the father. This rivalry embodies oedipal desires or conflicts to which the reader can respond. "Bantams in Pine-Woods" is generally recognized as a poem which presents a conflict. From an intellectual perspective, this conflict is interpreted as one between the personal imagination and the world of reality, or, even more abstractly, as a conflict between the personal and the universal. The personal and universal can be characterized more specifically in the poem and in such a way that its emotional significance becomes evident. The speaker, a bantam, is challenging another fowl called Chieftain Iffucan. All the descriptive adjectives which refer to Chieftain are meant to portray him as large and majestic. He is a chieftain; he is dressed in a full-length tunic, a caftan; he has long feathers, hackles; he is fat and portly; he is a ten-foot poet. As seen by the bantam, he is enormous: "Damned universal cock, as if the sun/Was blackamoor to bear your blazing tail." Chieftain seems so powerful, or so arrogant, that the sun is his servant. The bantam's view of Chieftain is similar to the child's view of the adult. The child at first sees the adult as omnipotent and enormous; the situation in the poem seems to present a small boy's view of his father. Iffucan is a chief, the father of his tribe, and, as a cock, is sexual. If the chief is large, a universal cock, the bantam, a diminutive fowl, is small. He characterizes himself as an inchling, and it should be noted that the word bantam also means a small, aggressive person; here, the bantam is aggressive toward the chief.

On all levels the poem presents a conflict between a small and large cock. The emotional content implies oedipal rivalry and hostility. The small bantam wants to be independent of the chieftain and to be free from his power. "Your world is you. I am my world." The bantam, as an aggressive person, expresses his hostility through curses, "damned universal

cock," and epithets, "Fat! Fat!" Just as the small boy wishes
his father to disappear, the bantam orders Chieftain to "be-
gone!" Just as the small boy wishes to replace the father and
assume the father's role, the bantam wishes to become universal cock:

> An inchling bristles in these pines,
>
> Bristles, and points their Appalachian tangs,
>
> And fears not portly Azcan nor his hoos.

The bantam, as an inchling, bristles. He is hostile and his
short hairs are erect. He points some kind of projection, tang,
phallic perhaps, and magnifies its size. It becomes moun-
tainous. Imagining himself enlarged, or as Chieftain, he
states that he no longer is afraid of the Chieftain. Finally, just
as the small boy wishes to be equal to the father, the bantam as
a son ("sun") no longer wants to be his servant: "as if the sun/
Was blackamoor to bear your blazing tail."

Whereas on one level, the poem presents a conflict between
the personal imagination and the world of reality (for Stevens
the naturalistic world we have previously discussed) on another, it is a conflict between the personal and the universal.
On still another, more emotional level, it embodies oedipal
hostility and rivalry. The poem presents clearly the relevant
emotions; what it obscures is the real subject. Connected to
the bantam is the small boy; connected to the ten-foot poet
and universal cock is the father. Though it attempts to obscure
the seriousness of the conflict behind a barrage of humourous
sound effects, the poem, in fact, presents a human cock fight.

In conclusion, Wallace Stevens, an apparently intellectual
and obtuse poet, can profitably be studied from a perspective
which takes into account the possibility of unconscious fantasies appearing in the poems. A major theme in his work, his
commitment to the natural world, seems also to embody oedipal fantasies. The image of the earth as a woman is associated
with the maternal, the naturalistic glorification of the earth is
sexualized, and comic conflicts can be interpreted as father-
son rivalries and battles. Looked at from another angle, these

strongly emotional oedipal concerns embodied in the poet's intellectual themes could explain why such intellectual and obscure poems could still have a significant impact on an ever-increasing number of readers, readers who themselves have struggled, to one extent or another, with oedipal concerns. As Stevens (1957) says in his *Adagia*, "We never arrive intellectually. But emotionally we arrive constantly" (p. 173).

# 9/THE AUTHOR:

# A Note
# on Wallace Stevens

Beginning with Freud, especially his work on Leonardo da Vinci (1910), the study of the relationship between the author's psyche and his creative product has been a popular area of endeavour. Jones (1955) attempted to connect Hamlet and Shakespeare. Most significant authors have been "psychoanalyzed." As I have argued elsewhere (Mollinger, 1975), such studies can be particularly productive when they (1) clarify a particular historical event, or the literary creation itself; (2) relate it to the particular, contemporary experience of the author while he was writing the work; and (3) understand the work and its contemporary framework in the light of earlier, childhood concerns. Such a study is, by necessity, speculative. The details one can accumulate in the psychoanalytic consulting room cannot be recaptured when years have passed, when the author is dead, and when one is at a far distance from the author, his unconscious, and his time.

Since continued exploration can eventually lead to further understanding, such limitations should not lead to the conclusion that psychoanalytic studies are worthless. With this in mind, and with the understanding that a look at psychic mechanisms does not imply a search for pathology, I shall isolate the biographical factors which seem to be relevant to the poems examined in the previous chapter. These poems, "Depression Before Spring," "Ploughing on Sunday," "Bantams in Pine-Woods," and "Hymn from a Watermelon Pavilion," all display Stevens's commitment to a natural, earthly world, a commitment which is founded on philosophic naturalism. I have argued, in Chapter 8, that in addition they display, and draw on, a particular emotional source — the oedipal complex.

Since little is known currently about Stevens's personal life, we can only speculate why these oedipal concerns appear, as we have seen in Chapter 8, in such a highly obscured, symbolic form in the poems. Most of the poems discussed appear in *Harmonium*, the volume which both established the poet's interests and concerns for his lifetime. This book set forth his themes most explicitly so that a brief glance at Stevens's personal life at the time he was writing *Harmonium* might be profitable. *Harmonium* was first published in 1923; however, most of the poems it contained, especially those discussed here, were written during the preceding years. "Depression Before Spring" was written in 1918; "Ploughing on Sunday" in 1919; and "Bantams in Pine-Woods" and "Hymn From a Watermelon Pavilion" in 1922. Stevens's marital life during these years, or what we know of it, is of interest. Married in 1909 at the age of thirty to Elsie Kachel, Stevens in the years following his marriage was frequently separated from his wife for extended periods. On account of her health, Elsie spent each summer from 1910 to 1916 vacationing alone in various parts of Pennsylvania. The couple was not only separated during the summers; working in the New York office of the American Bonding Company and then later in Hartford for the Hartford Live Stock Insurance Company, Stevens was required to take numerous business trips. His letters indicate that in 1916 he was in St. Paul in March, Atlanta and Miami in April, Albany in May, St. Paul again in

June, and Omaha in September. Though Elsie's separate vacations ended in 1916, Stevens continued to travel. In 1917 he was in Houston, in 1918 during March and April in Indianapolis, Chicago, and Tennessee, in 1919 through 1922 in Florida for extended periods, and in 1923 in Cuba. Not until 1923 did Stevens take his first extended vacation with his wife, fourteen years after their marriage. It was during this first vacation, from October 18, 1923 to approximately December 11, 1923, that Stevens's first and only child, Holly (born August 10, 1924), was conceived; Stevens was almost forty-five at the time.

Until this vacation in 1923, the Stevens' marital life was marked by continual separations. These separations may have caused long periods of sexual abstinence. The lack of a child for fifteen years is at least one small sign in support of this view. The curious fact that Holly was conceived during the first vacation the couple spent together is perhaps another. The possible abstinence of Stevens during the period from 1909 to late 1923 may have led to the emergence of sexual desires and masturbatory fantasies in the poems written during these years and published in *Harmonium* in 1923.

There is even less evidence available to construct an hypothesis to explain a possible regression to incestual material in the fantasies embodied in the poems, but the poet's letters and journal entries provide some interesting and relevant material. Writing from a country visit to his mother in 1895 at the age of sixteen, he expressed a desire to return home immediately, apparently because he could find no male companionship. The men were occupying their time with young women. Stevens was not interested: "I hate *ladies?* (such as are here). [They] are all agreeable enough but familiarity breeds contempt — poor deluded females — they are contemptible without familiarity" (Stevens, 1966, p. 5). Having found the young women unattractive, Stevens shows a continuing attachment to his mother by wanting to return home to her. He told her that he would come home the very evening on the day he receives her answering letter.

Perhaps more revealing are endings in Stevens's letters to his mother. A letter dated July 23, 1895, romantically ends "I can be your own dearest tootsey wootsey." The ending of his next letter dated August 4, 1895, merges Stevens's relation to his mother with his father's: "I am not one of [the] Bacchanalians however — but with love to yourself — yourself's partner and you and your partner's remaining assets I myself am as ever, Yours truly Wallace Stevens" (p. 7). The "partner" seems to refer first to Stevens and then to his father. He is her partner just as his father is. This oedipal implication is almost hidden by the same defensive obscurity seen in the poems and by the extreme formality of his ending signature.

The ending of the next letter dated August 12, 1895, seems to imply a sexual undertone to the boy's relation with his mother: "(I have a ten foot pimple on my nose.)" There seems here a phallic symbol upon a phallic symbol. Finally, in a letter to his mother the following year, Stevens ended by saying "Forever with supernal affection, thy rosy-lipped archangelic jeune." Stevens, red-lipped, refers to himself as a *jeune*. The first meaning in French of *jeune* is that of a young, unripe or unfulfilled man; there is a hint here of sexual incompletion. A subsidiary meaning (*jeune premier*) is of an actor who takes lover's parts. Here, again, is a sexual implication. Finally, a similar word — *jeûne* — means abstinence; again, a reference to unfulfilled love. Stevens writes to his mother that he is a passionate ("red-lipped") young man who loves her but is unfulfilled. These letter endings (Stevens, 1966) show the revival of oedipal fantasies which need to be further worked through. Under the later stress of possible abstinence, these fantasies are apparently again revived and appear in the poetry.

From 1898 to 1912, the year of his mother's death, Stevens kept a Journal (Stevens, 1966). In it, under the date of February 20, 1901, is the outline of a plot for a play, one which apparently was never finished. Here is a brief synopsis of the plot of *Olivia: A Romantic Comedy* in Stevens's words:

Olivia Rainbow, an American, is visiting France with her brother Harry. She goes to Dijon . . . to spend a few days in the chateau of the Duke of Bellemer, a friend of Harry's. There she encounters, besides the Duke, three Frenchmen who fall madly in love with her. . . . She appears to encourage each of the three. (One of the three is a poet.) . . . Their conduct plainly shows that they are in love — the Duke's does not. . . . [An arrangement is made whereby] whichever of the three shall knock a leaf or flower or something off her shoulder (?) shall have the privilege of at least one rendezvous with her where he may speak for himself. . . . The first knocks off the flower; the second also; the poet fails — Olivia jabs and pokes him. . . . makes him ridiculous. (p. 51)

Through a series of mistakes, the first two Frenchmen do not keep their rendezvous; the poet is finally rejected; and Olivia marries the Duke.

There are parallels between the plot outline and Stevens's family situation. Just as there are three Frenchmen, there were three sons in Stevens's family, Garrett, Wallace and John. Just as one Frenchman was a poet, one son, Wallace, was a poet. Olivia may represent Stevens's mother, for in the end she marries the Duke, whose superior status gives him the aura of a father-figure. The three sons who woo the (apparently seductive) mother fail, especially the poet-son Wallace. In this play Stevens makes the poet, the stereotyped lover, French, just as he made himself the French lover of his mother in his letters, the rosy-lipped *jeune*. This outline of a drama seems transparently symbolic of Stevens's oedipus complex. Perhaps in his later poetry this material arises in a more obscured, symbolic form. From the perspective of Stevens's personal life, these fantasies seem to have been revived in periods of stress, in his letters in adolescence and in his poetry during a period of possible abstinence.

# 10/THE AUTHOR:

# Edgar Allan Poe

Intrigued and fascinated by the mystery, horror, and extra-ordinary occurrences of Edgar Allan Poe's poems and tales, readers and literary critics alike have speculated on the relationship between the author's psychological makeup and his writings. It has been thought that he was a frustrated actor, that he had an unsatisfactory home life, that he had too much freedom when young, that he was possessed by a devil or demon, that he inherited a moral disease, that he was an alcoholic or a drug addict, or that he had a brain lesion or epilepsy (Young, 1951). From a psychoanalytic perspective, Bonaparte (1949) in her full-length study of Poe's life and works pays particular attention to the oedipal aspects of his psyche — his attachment to his mother and his revolt against, and submission to, his father. With the more recent psychoanalytic exploration of the child's earliest months and years, it is now possible to hypothesize about the traumatic effect preoedipal events in Poe's childhood might have had on those concerns evident in his literary works.

Born on January 19, 1809, to David Poe, an alcoholic actor, and Elizabeth Arnold Poe, a tubercular actress, Edgar

Allan Poe was soon to endure separation after separation from the significant people in his life. First, when he was one and one-half years old, his father deserted the family. Then, a sister Rosalie was born in December, 1810, just before Poe was two years old. This undoubtedly took some of his be-leaguered mother's attention away from him. Soon after, in the summer of 1811, Elizabeth Arnold became seriously ill with tuberculosis, a disease which further limited her care of her son during that year. In December, she died. Poe was just under three years of age. Subsequently, he underwent further losses which, we may presume, revived the death of his mother and solidified its significance. Taken in by John and Frances Allan, Poe found in Frances a new loving mother but in John a hateful, rejecting father. Apparently John Allan never really desired a son but only was attempting to please his wife by taking in the boy. When Poe was seventeen, Allan cut him off financially and prevented him from returning to college. Frances died in 1829 when Poe was only twenty. John, continuing his poor treatment, refused to inform Poe so that he could be at her bedside.

Somewhat earlier, at age fifteen, Poe had already lost an-other woman close to him, the older Mrs. Stanard who had encouraged his literary talent. Abandoned by his real father at one and a half and by his foster father at seventeen, Poe also lost his real mother at three, a substitute mother at fifteen, and his foster mother at twenty. For Poe, abandonment and loss was a central issue in his life.

Though Poe lost his father first, important as such a trauma may be, it was probably not the most significant in his life, since a father is not the most important figure to an infant at that age. The absence of his father might have hindered young Poe's identification as a male, caused him to distrust men, provoked him to prove his masculinity and led him to have little control over his impulses (Biller, 1971). But it must be remembered that in John Allan, he did later have a male figure in the house. The father's desertion must, of course, have affected Poe's mother, and, in turn, her treatment of the infant Poe. Distraught over her husband's desertion, she may have turned to other men. More importantly, she now had to care for Poe on her own. Though it might be possible to trace the influence of some, or all, of these external complications on Poe's psyche and on his creative work, I suspect that the death of Poe's mother is, by and large, much more important to his psychic development, especially in the context of the other losses he experienced.

Poe lost his mother at a time (before three years of age) particularly important to the infant's psychic growth. Poe by this time had become strongly attached to her as the one who satisfied his needs. Because of the lack of maturity of the psychic apparatus, such a young child cannot yet fully differentiate his image of himself from his image of his mother. To such a child, his mother is not a separate person; they are rather a dual unity, two people as one. Most intense when the infant is six months old, this unity slowly begins to dissolve, and the infant begins to distinguish himself from his mother. By thirty-six months he begins to see himself as a separate person. This differentiation is predicated on all going well at this time of growth. As we have seen, all did not go well for Poe during this period. I suggest that at the time Poe lost his mother he had not yet formed an image of himself as a whole, separate person. He had probably mastered several psychic steps on the way to such an image: he could see himself as good, capable of being satisfied, and his mother as good, capable of satisfying. It is likely that when he had a bad experience he could not distinguish between his own bad feeling, such as frustration, and the cause of that feeling, that his mother might have frustrated him. Thus, in feeling bad, frustrated, or tense, it is possible that he still imagined in his mind, not himself as bad or his mother as bad, but rather both, a dual unity, as bad. He had probably not yet integrated his image of himself into a person who could be both good (satisfied) and bad (frustrated), nor his image of his mother into a separate person who could both satisfy and frustrate. For instance, a person who has been rejected by a lover may feel totally unlovable, forgetting the many times of acceptance by a lover. From another point of view, a patient may see me as kindly until I deny a request; at that point, I am seen only as one who deprives; all memory of me as one who gives is forgotten.

When a child loses his mother at this point in his development, numerous reactions can occur. These reactions might become evident in later creative work. For some, such a loss can lead to a depression. Bowlby (1969) has illustrated how, after a certain period without the mother, the child gives up hope of her return and descends into apathy. Recent work (Brazelton and Stern, 1977) also has shown how young infants go limp in reaction to an immobile, nonresponsive mother. Poe must have endured this situation while his mother lay dying.

Earlier, in Chapter 4, I argued that Roderick Usher is depressed, despondent from the expected loss of his dearly beloved sister. Just as Poe lost a love object, Usher loses a love object. Since I have already examined extensively this depressive mechanism in "The Fall of the House of Usher," further exploration of the manifestation of depressive mechanisms in Poe's works is unnecessary here.

There are other important reactions a child under three years old experiences when abandoned. First, the loss induces rage. Before he becomes depressed, the child, under the stress of being separated from his mother, will be furious and scream; soon after, if she returns, he will give her the angry "silent treatment." Secondly, he will attempt to handle the abandonment imaginatively. To maintain the tie to the abandoning other, the child fuses his internal self-image with the internal image of the good mother. From his perspective, since he cannot distinguish the mother as a whole person, it is the bad mother who has left, not the good one. If one becomes unified with the other person, then one can control what is happening and one's rage. As Rose (1972) puts it in speaking of a patient,

> In an effort to protect herself from the intense anxiety of these experiences, she developed vivid fantasies of fusing with her surroundings. . . . She explained that if everything were really herself, she could, by fusing with it, control the amount of hurt she administered or received. Merging . . . was thus an attempt to defend herself against . . . massive aggressivization. . . . if she invested herself in everything she would have control and thus wouldn't need to be afraid of assaulting or being assaulted by everything. (p. 180)

Related to this fusion, is the constant seeking of an object or other to unite with. In order to control the rage against the bad, the abandoning other person, the child idealizes the other he seeks to merge with. If the other is perfect and one merges with the other, one becomes perfect himself and thereby safe.

I suggest, then, that Poe was traumatically affected by the loss of his mother at age two years and eleven months, that he might have had typical reactions — such as depression, rage, a desire for fusion with the idealized other — to such a loss. I suggest, further, that these reactions become matters of concern in his later writings. We have seen earlier how depression is of major importance in "The Fall of the House of Usher"; here I shall examine how the twin elements rage and a desire to be united with the idealized other person are manifested in Poe's tales.

Numerous tales by Poe, such as "The Tell-Tale Heart" and "The Cask of Amontillado," concern murder and hate, but "Berenice" and "The Black Cat" especially show how rage is connected to abandonment and loss in the author's works.

"Berenice" concerns the effect of the beautiful Berenice on her cousin, the narrator. Generally gloomy and ill, the narrator is brought to some sense of joy by his "agile, graceful" cousin, that is, until she too becomes ill. The narrator reacts by becoming still more ill himself: "In the meantime my own disease . . . grew rapidly upon me, and assumed finally a monomaniac character. . . ." Consisting of an obsessive attentiveness to trivia, this kind of obsessiveness, psychoanalyti-

cally understood, serves to keep one's mind off disturbing
feelings. The narrator constantly reminds us that he is a man
of the head and not of the heart. "In the strange anomaly of
my existence, feelings with me *had never been* of the heart,
and my passions *always were* of the mind" (Poe's italics).
Amusing himself by fantasizing, dreaming, and having visions, as well as by his obsession with the frivolous, he deni-
grates any emotion. "I called to mind that she loved me long,
and, in an evil moment, I spoke to her of marriage." For the
narrator, to express affection is evil. As Berenice becomes
"lifeless" and the narrator avoids his feelings, his monomania
fixates on her teeth: "For these I longed with a frenzied desire." He sees them everywhere. Ignoring everything else, he
examines, in his imagination, their every detail and experiences "fury," "horror," and "dismay." Finally Berenice dies
and is buried. All too soon the narrator has intimations that he
has done something horrible. Not knowing exactly what he
has done, he needs the help of a household menial to discover
it:

> He told of a wild cry disturbing the silence of the night — of the
> gathering together of the household — of a search in the direc-
> tion of the sound; — and then his tones grew thrillingly distinct
> as he whispered to me of a violated grave — of a disfigured
> body enshrouded, yet still breathing, still palpitating, still
> *alive*.
> He pointed to my garments; — they were muddy and clotted
> with gore. I spoke not, and he took me gently by the hand; — it
> was indented with the impress of human nails. He directed my
> attention to some object against the wall; — I looked at it for
> some minutes; — it was a spade. With a shriek I bounded to the
> table, and grasped the box that lay upon it. But I could not
> force it open; and in my tremor it slipped from my hands, and
> fell heavily, and burst into pieces; and from it, with a rattling
> sound, there rolled out some instruments of dental surgery,
> intermingled with thirty-two small, white and ivory-looking
> substances that were scattered to and fro about the floor.

Having ripped the teeth out of an apparently still-living Berenice, the narrator has violated, disfigured, and mutilated her. His obsessive monomania had kept in check a "fury," a fury which results in rageful violence against Berenice.

Looking again through the story, we can find the provocation for this rage. First, "a fatal disease" strikes Berenice, just when the narrator had some hopes for joy in his life. At the moment he realizes that Berenice will no longer be the Berenice he once knew, his monomania concerning trivia begins. Her expected demise and his obsessiveness are thus connected. Secondly, as his wedding day approaches, and with it an expected closeness to Berenice, she enters his library. He notices that she is becoming more and more lifeless. Just at this moment, as he explores her decaying face, he focuses his attention on her teeth. The specific fixation of his monomania is here connected to her expected death. Thirdly, the obsession over the teeth actually begins when she physically leaves the narrator:

> The shutting of the door disturbed me, and, looking up, I found that my cousin had departed from the chamber. But from the disordered chamber of my brain, had not, alas! departed, and would not be driven away, the white and ghastly *spectrum* of the teeth.

Finally, of course, the actual gory violence occurs after Berenice is buried and thought to be gone for good. All these indicate that the obsession with the teeth and the rage enacted on Berenice are stimulated by the contemplated and actual loss of Berenice. This separation from Berenice leads to the narrator's rage.

There are several intimations of autobiographical material in "Berenice." In the story, first published in 1835, the narrator is planning to marry his cousin, who (apparently) dies in her youth. In reality, in 1835, Poe married his cousin Virginia, who was sickly and died at the age of twenty-five. In addition, it has often been noted that Poe's experience with

Virginia parallels that with his mother Elizabeth Arnold. Both women are sickly, both die young, and both leave him alone, without them. The fictive cousin Berenice is related to the real cousin Virginia who, in turn, is related to the real mother. Appropriately, the importance of the mother is hinted at in the story. In speaking of his youthful gloom, the narrator, apparently for no reason, mentions his mother: "Here died my mother. Herein was I born." The implication is that his mother's death is relevant to his melancholy and to what follows in the story. What we can more assuredly conclude exist are striking parallels between the story and Poe's life and that separation, loss, and death are essential aspects of each. In the mutilation of Berenice, the story demonstrates the rage experienced at the time of such losses.

That this theme is more than an aberration in Poe's work can be seen by a study of "The Black Cat." Describing himself as docile and tender, the narrator, in his actual behavior, demonstrates his ruthlessness. Proclaiming his love of animals and of his wife, he kills his pet cat Pluto, attempts to kill a second pet cat, and puts an axe in his wife's head. Though the narrator ascribes to alcohol the beginning of this rage, which included "intemperate language" and "violence" to his wife, there is an actual incident which sets off the killings.

> One night, returning home, much intoxicated, from one of my haunts about town, I fancied that the cat avoided my presence. I seized him. . . .

He then proceeds to cut out its eye and later, his fury unsatisfied, to hang it. Interestingly enough, it is the avoidance by the cat which provokes the narrator. The feeling of abandonment leads to his murderous rage. Not being able to tolerate being without a cat, the narrator is then led to replace it: "I went . . . to look about me . . . for another pet of the same species, and of somewhat similar appearance, with which to supply its place." The stress here is on filling the gap, the "place," left by the dead pet. Having not yet exhausted his rage over the first cat's avoidance of him, the narrator's aversion to the new cat increases until he goes after it with an axe.

The symbolism of the cat now emerges clearly. Throughout the story the cat has been connected to women. Black cats are regarded as witches, and the second cat, which has taken to the wife immediately, has a white milky splotch on its breast. In addition, the term "pussy," or cat, has universally been symbolically representative of the female genitals. This second cat, found in a "den of more than infamy," is seen as an evil woman. It is a real witch with an image of death, "the gallows," on its breast, and its milk is like poison. The narrator remarks, "I came to look upon it with unutterable loathing, and to flee silently from its odious presence, as from the breath of a pestilence." Having first directed his violence toward his wife verbally, he displaced that violence onto the first cat. Now, when he goes after the second cat and his wife stops him, he puts the axe in her skull. His real target has emerged. Symbolically, this avoiding cat is an avoiding woman, an abandoning one.

Whereas in "Berenice" and "The Black Cat" murderous fury is horribly enacted, other stories show ways of limiting such fury. The rage provoked by abandonments can be controlled by an attempted imaginative merger with another. If a person is able to fuse with others, especially idealized others, he cannot be left by them and need not be enraged. Through such a merger he becomes safe and powerful himself. Numerous Poe tales illustrate this dynamic. In "The Fall of the House of Usher," the characters, including the House itself, are all mirror reflections of each other (see Chapter 4). Elsewhere (Mollinger, R. and Mollinger, S., 1977) I argue that a similar fusion of identities of the narrator, the portrait, the artist, and even Poe, takes place in "The Oval Portrait." In "The Tell-Tale Heart" the narrator mistakes his own beating heart for that of the dead man he killed. From a slightly different perspective, "Berenice" has shown us the longing for the lost object which provokes such fusion, a unity which recaptures what is lost. As Berenice dies, the narrator madly covets her teeth: "I felt that their possession could alone ever restore me to peace." As she leaves him, he needs to keep a part of her, which he aggressively takes. Called a "sylph" and a "Naiad," Berenice is the longed-for idealized woman. "Oh! gorgeous yet fantastic beauty!" and Poe, of course, idealizes most women — Annabel Lee is envied by angels and Eulalie is more radiant than stars.

It is the story "Ligeia," however, which best illustrates the merger with the lost, idealized other and its relation to abandonment and rage. Her paternity unknown, her beauty unequalled, her demeanour majestic, her "spirit-lifting vision" "wildly divine," and her eyes "divine orbs," Ligeia is magnified to an immortal. Her learning is "immense" and "gigantic." "I said her knowledge was such as I have never known in woman — but where breathes the man who has traversed, and successfully, *all* the wide areas of moral, physical, and mathematical science?" She has brought to the narrator material wealth, "far more, very far more than ordinarily falls to the lot of mortals." Ligeia is a goddess; to the narrator, she is everything.

Such extreme idealization comes from ambivalence; it protects the other person (and the self) from intense hatred. For example, one of my patients continually pointed out how helpful, wise, intelligent, and educated I was, while beneath this attitude was one of contempt and scorn. Another patient, upon meeting me on the street, wanted to say proudly to someone "That's my psychotherapist!" During the same period, he was imaging me in his dreams as a weak woman. Likewise, in "Ligeia" contempt and hate quickly emerge when Ligeia dies. "Crushed into the very dust with sorrow," with Ligeia's money the narrator buys an abbey in a desolate, wild region of England. He pinpoints his motivation exactly: "the feelings of utter abandonment which had driven me into that remote and unsocial region of the country." Feeling abandoned by the dead Ligeia, he replaces her with Lady Rowena, whom he despises. He gives her a chamber which is full of monstrosities and has a "hideous and uneasy animation." Continuing to idealize and love Ligeia, for no apparent reason he passionately hates Rowena.

> I loathed her with a hatred belonging more to a demon than to a man. My memory flew back (oh, with what intensity of regret!) to Ligeia, the beloved, the august, the beautiful, the entombed. I revelled in recollections  of her purity, of her wisdom, her ethereal nature. . . .

To protect Ligeia, the ideal, good person, from his murderous rage, this rage is directed totally toward another person, Rowena. Appropriately enough, the narrator poisons Rowena. "I became distinctly aware of a gentle footfall upon the carpet. . . . I saw, fall within the goblet, as if from some invisible spring in the atmosphere of the room, three or four large drops of a brilliant and ruby-coloured fluid." Soon after, Rowena dies. Just as in "Berenice," the narrator is unaware of his violent act. Here the narrator acts as if a mysterious force poisoned Rowena, even though he is the only person in the room when the crime is committed. He then imagines that Ligeia returns in the body of Rowena: "And now slowly opened *the eyes* of the figure which stood before me. . . . I shrieked 'the Lady Ligeia!' " In his imagination the idealized, good other person has returned to replace the denigrated, bad one. With good replacing bad, love can replace hate, and the desire for the lost idealized love is fulfilled. Since we never see what these women are really like, it is clear that these images of the women are in the narrator's mind: both the idealized one of Ligeia and the denigrated one of Rowena. Earlier in the story the narrator had mentally fused himself with the image of the good other, "Ligeia's beauty passed into my spirit," and now, with the elimination of the bad Rowena, he can do this again. Fantasizing the imagined return of Ligeia and the end of his abandonment, he can give up his rage.

The story is, of course, reminiscent of Poe's life: the demise of Ligeia in the story strikingly parallels the abandonment of Poe by Elizabeth Arnold when she dies. Elsewhere (Mollinger, R. and Mollinger, S., 1977) I have argued that, in "The Oval Portrait," the woman character is a replica of Elizabeth Arnold. Bonaparte (1949) has attempted to make the same comparison with Ligeia, particularly in regard to her slender figure and the make-up of her face. She notes how Poe went to his foster mother Frances Allan after the death of Elizabeth Arnold and how the narrator goes to Rowena after the death of Ligeia. She has a view, similar to mine, of the main component of the story: "Thus, does Poe unwittingly declare, that every later love from Frances Allan to Virginia and her successors, would never be other than a reincarnation of his first undying love for his mother—still living in his unconscious—and ever to be reactivated by each new passion" (p. 235). Though biography is helpful here, it is not necessary. The story itself indicates that the relationship of the narrator to Ligeia is one of child and mother. Idealizing Ligeia, the narrator submits to her teachings: "I was sufficiently aware of her infinite supremacy to resign myself, with a childlike confidence, to her guidance. . . ." His perspective parallels the young child who sees his mother as omniscient and omnipotent. Later, when Ligeia dies, he reacts like a helpless child. "Without Ligeia I was but as a child groping benighted." Feeling abandoned, he attempts to alleviate his sorrow with "a childlike perversity." It is understandable why he longs so for the lost Ligeia; he is as helpless without her as a child who has lost his mother.

To conclude, these stories show a major concern with loss: death and abandonment. The expected emotional reactions also appear: rage and a longing for a fusion with the idealized lost one. Significantly, throughout his life and especially in his childhood, Poe experienced numerous losses: his mothers by death, his fathers by emotional abandonment.

# 11/THE READER:

# Personality
# and Preference

The exploration of the reader's response to literature begins
with Freud (1909) who stated that literature allows the reader
to enjoy forbidden fantasies. Developing Freud's idea, Kris
(1951) holds that the reader also attempts to control these
fantasies so that reading involves an interchange between
writer's and reader's fantasies and their modes of control.
Drawing on Kris, Holland (1975b) dwells more exclusively on
what the reader brings to the literary text and how he re-
creates that text. Holland finds that the reader reads according to his identity. He finds his own fantasies in the text and
transforms them to more intellectually significant meanings.
Taking the final subjectivist step, Bleich (1975–1976) states
that the reader creates meaning as if the text did not exist. In
an attempt to be more encompassing and more objective, S.
Mollinger (1978) explores the interrelations between the literary text, its author and his culture, and the reader. All these
critics approach the problem of how readers find meaning in
literature.

I shall look at a closely related, but possibly preceding, step:
how a reader chooses what to read. Whereas much of the

exploration of the reader's response has used for data psychological test results of the reader, I shall use the discoveries of the psychoanalytic therapeutic situation of three patients. I shall suggest "who these patients are," that is, those elements of their identities which influence their selection of reading matter and illuminate their perspective on what they read.

A., a young artist, is generally sociable and pleasant with her friends. Despite having little money — she lives financially from day to day — she serves them expensive dinners. Buying only the best ingredients, she works for days preparing numerous courses — quiches, soups, lamb, mousse, and pies. What concerns her most at these dinners is the ambience of the setting and the feeling that she is entertaining her friends lavishly. Creating a myth of not being poor, she spends money as if she does not need it. She buys herself expensive clothes and sends her daughter to an excellent, but costly, private school. Although poor in reality, in fantasy she is rich.

This mode of behavior is expressed in relation to me as well. She fantasizes about having tea with me in the therapy sessions, of entertaining me with stories, and of having me tell her stories as well. Once she brought me flowers. Particularly liking the fact that I am interested in the poetry of Wallace Stevens, she feels that it shows that I have "taste." She also enjoys socializing with another psychologist and his wife, particularly because they often have musical recitals in their home.

A. was reared by second-generation Americans with an Eastern European background. From her mother's point of view, her father and his family were lower-class brutes: they wore undershirts around the house, ate like pigs, and were generally slobs. In contrast, A.'s mother was interested in music, ballet, and "culture" and saw herself as a person of "higher quality." In A.'s estimation, her mother had aristocratic pretensions, even though it was her mother who introduced A. to all these cultural aspects of life. A. now has similar attitudes. Imitating her mother, A. views most of the men she dates as "brutes" and feels herself to be much above them, especially culturally.

A. tries to actualize the myth of wealth and culture in order to obtain approval and love from others. She romanticizes herself and others to protect herself from the realization of her feelings of unworthiness and of her fear of rejection because of this unworthiness. She serves her friends lavish dinners to obtain their approval; she brings me flowers so I will like her. In a dream, she dresses in a gray suit and stockings, as a "lady," for me, while at the same time she hopes I would dress better, more like a "gentleman." Another dream further illustrates her reason for carrying her "cultural baggage." In it, her former husband was going to take her away from her parents; meanwhile, she looked frantically for her books and paintings. Discussing the dream, she said that without these, she might not be good enough to be accepted by someone. She thinks that her husband would only love her if she has cultural interests. In addition, from A.'s perspective, her mother could only accept her, and she could only accept herself, if she was "highly cultured."

A.'s fantasy of herself is, then, of a young wealthy hostess who lavishly entertains her friends, who socializes with the culturally superior who enjoy music and art, and who at times must be victimized by the company of those beneath her, the brutes of the world. In her own eyes, she is a young, intelligent *bon vivant*.

It is suggestive that her favorite author is Henry James. Though she appreciates the complex psychological explorations in his works, they do not interest her. Though she is well travelled, the international plots and the contrast between America and Europe do not fascinate her. Though she loves to curl up with detective novels, the Jamesian mystery and ghost stories do not intrigue her. Though she is sensitive to her own psychic dynamics, James's focus on the self and "selfishness," does not strike her. What draws her primarily to the novels of Henry James is the ambience of "ladies" and "gentlemen."

The afternoon teas, the social dinners, the distinctive "manners," the politeness, the ever presence of wealth and leisure, these are the aspects of James's work which particularly entrance A.

The opening of *The Portrait of a Lady* (1881) illustrates this kind of ambience: "Under certain circumstances there are few hours in life more agreeable than the hour dedicated to the ceremony known as afternoon tea." Present in the scene of the novel are, among others, an American banker, an expatriate and an English gentleman with "the air of a happy temperament fertilized by a high civilization — which would have made almost any observer envy him at a venture. . . ." The conversation turns to leisured comfort:

> "The fact is I've been comfortable so many years that I suppose I've got so used to it I don't know it."
> "Yes, that's the bore of comfort," said Lord Warburton. "We only know when we're uncomfortable."

The talk then turns to wealth: "You think too much of your pleasure. You're too fastidious, and too indolent, and too rich."

The elements in this scene are typically Jamesian, wealth, leisure, comfort, all symbolized by the taking of tea. Whenever A. is in distress, she loves to treat herself to a "calming cup of tea." It composes her, especially by stimulating her fantasy of herself in such a Jamesian scene: not poor but rich, not chaotic but calm, not lower middle class but aristocratic. Besides having tea to calm herself, she retreats to bed to read James, particularly after a narcissistic injury (either a social or professional rejection). She has said, "I'm like a lower-class English person who likes to read of nobility. I identify with people who have grace, money, a library, a comfortable chair by the window, success." Though she sometimes reads detective novels, she worries that others, particularly me, will think that she has "bad" taste in literature. Of course, reading these "lesser works" also dents her fantasy of being "cultured."

I am suggesting that A.'s fantasy of herself — a restorative fantasy for her injured self-esteem, one which makes her feel more worthwhile after a rejection — influences her choice of James's works, especially since she reads him after being rejected or slighted. This relationship can also be understood by Holland's (1968) thesis that the reader finds his own defenses in the literary text. We have something additional here, the active seeking of reading material which buttresses a restorative, defensive fantasy. Reading James's scenes of manners, A. becomes a part of them, and acceptable to herself and to (imagined) others, such as her mother and me.

B., a creative young college student who composes and sings his own songs, also has a special interest in literature. When young, he was generally ignored or beaten. Sent away to a special school when he was two years old, he later attended a prep school far from home. Even at home, his parents were self-involved and paid little attention to him. One way B. handled this deprivation and rejection was to withdraw into his own fantasies. He constructed a huge model city and gave it his own name, spelled backward. He imagined himself a king of England with a castle and pictured himself on Mount Olympus. Now, he fantasizes himself as a famous entertainer surrounded by other "deities" of the entertainment world. One of his dreams shows his fortressed position:

> I'm in a castle. I was near the top.
> President Ford fell out of the window
> and got killed. I was offered the Presidency.

There is, of course, aggression and grandiosity here, but in addition there is a separateness, in the castle, and an immersion in the fantasy itself. B. feels as if there is a barrier between himself and others. Whereas A. used her fantasy at particular times, B. lives in his fantasy world most of the time. The actualization of this fantasy of grandiose success guides most of what he does: his writing, reading, and sexual behavior. Totally involved in these fantasies, he experiences them as a major element in his personality.

It is suggestive that what he reads and writes captures the ambience of his fantasies. He writes romantic, fantastical songs which have nothing to do with contemporary life or contemporary problems. He succeeds in putting himself at a distance from the life around him by going back toward the past. In reading literature, he chooses medieval works, like *Beowulf,* or science fiction (again far removed from the present), or literature that creates its own strange world, such as works by H. D. Lovecraft or Edgar Allan Poe:

> I entered the Gothic archway of the hall. . . . While the objects around me — while the carvings of the ceilings, the somber tapestries of the walls, the ebon blackness on the floors, and the phantasmagoric armorial trophies which rattled as I strode, were but matters to which, or to such as which, I had been accustomed from my infancy — while I hesitated not to acknowledge how familiar was all this — I still wondered to find how unfamiliar were the fancies which ordinary images were stirring up. ("The Fall of the House of Usher")

Although the narrator hesitates to enter this other-worldly gothic environment, B. has no hesitancy. This is just the kind of world he loves to enter, one cut off from everyday reality and everyday concerns. In his sexual behavior, he is particularly drawn to the "mysterious" and grotesque back rooms and bathhouses of the homosexual world.

In B. we again see the influence of a psychic dynamic on the choice of reading matter. B. has been constructing such fantastical worlds since childhood, the city of his own name, his kingdom on Mount Olympus, his kingdom in England. His immersion in those earlier, created fantasies is now paralleled by his immersion in literature which presents worlds far removed from the ordinary — other planets (science fiction), other historical periods (*Beowulf*), and other atmospheres (gothic). Having originally withdrawn from his childhood reality, he now withdraws from contemporary life and from a literature involved with contemporary reality. He summed this up by saying, "I write escapist lyrics and poems and they come from when I was young and living in a world of magic and marvels."

C., a graduate student in literature who had a rigid Catholic upbringing, fears authority figures and dreads being abandoned by his lovers. To handle these fears he attempts to please others, but at times he is compelled to defy them. This increases his anxious expectation of punishment and abandonment. Overwhelmed by anxiety and rage, C. attempts to control these emotions by the use of his mind. In therapy he continually looks for patterns and connections to what he is saying, while in his everyday life, he attempts to make the "perfect decision." As he puts it, "If I'm rational, I won't crap up."

One of his dreams shows the necessity for control and the danger of loss of control. In the dream he was committing hari kari, but he had the thought that it would be too messy. So, not wanting anyone to know, he stopped. In associating to the dream, he said that during the day he felt he had to clean some messy spots off his suit jacket before seeing his departmental chairman. He said that his former wife and his mother, who were continually cleaning their respective houses, would always criticize him for spilling milk. This criticism caused him to feel that he had to hide his mess from them to avoid their anger. In thinking of hari kari, he stated that the Japanese believe the stomach is the seat of the emotions. He believed that he had to protect himself from the reaction of others to his "messiness," a messiness caused by opening himself up and showing his emotions.

Stressing his need to control, to intellectualize, and to use his rational powers continually, he often noted the appropriateness of his choices in literature. His major is eighteenth-century literature. Alexander Pope's "Essay on Man" (1733–1734), a representative eighteenth-century work, strikingly displays similar emphases. For Pope, the world is orderly: "throughout the whole visible world, an universal order . . . is observed." Poetically put, "Order is Heaven's first law. . . ." For C., order is his "first law," what he needs and what he seeks for protection against all the minor disruptions and irregularities disturbing him.

Pope recommends that man submit to the order of the Universe: "Heaven bestows on thee./Submit." If one submits, one will be rewarded: "Who sees and follows that great scheme the best,/Best knows the blessing, and will be most blessed." To defy the order is to commit a sin: "And who but wishes to invert the laws/Of order, sins against th' Eternal Cause." In similar case, C. feels he must submit to others, their demands, their "orders," their authority. If he does, he will be rewarded—by being liked, by not being abandoned, by being considered "good." In youth, he submitted to the Church; now he submits to more mundane authority figures. Even though defiance is "bad," he commits acts of defiance by "sinfully" living with a woman to whom he is not married, by not paying me for his therapy sessions, a defiance which to his mind might lead to my "cancelling him out," thereby both abandoning and destroying him.

For Pope, the way to submission to order is through reason, "to reason right is to submit." Reason is man's finest capacity, "reason alone countervails all other faculties." For C., also, it is reason which will save him from his own messy emotions, from the messiness which might result from conflicts with other people. He feels pressure to make "perfect" decisions, to say the "right" thing to me and other authority figures, and to find his psychological patterns "healthy." To achieve these goals, he is constantly thinking, reasoning, and mulling things over. He feels that if he thinks enough, he will find the right solutions, however long it may take.

In summary, we see how readers respond to literature in terms of their own fantasies and defenses. Fantasizing herself as culturally and aristocratically superior, A. concentrates on the leisured aristocratic aspects of James's works. Defending himself by constructing his own fantasy world, B. creates in his own works fantastical worlds and seeks the same in literature: historical, science fiction, or gothic. Defending himself against his messy emotions, C. uses his rationality to create order in his world, even if it means submitting to some ultimate authoritative order. He seeks such a reasoned, ordered world in his professional commitment to literature.

These readers not only find themselves in what they read, but they actively seek out themselves in literature. They use their literary interests to strengthen their defenses against what upsets them — recognition of unworthiness in A., contact with others in B., and emotionality in C.

# Bibliography

Alexander, F. *Fundamentals of Psychoanalysis*. New York: W. W. Norton, 1948.

Arieti, S. *Creativity: The Magic Synthesis*. New York: Basic Books, 1976.

Axelrod, S. and Brody, S. *Anxiety and Ego Formation in Infancy*. New York: International Universities Press, 1970.

Benamou, M. "Le Thème du héros dans la poésie de Wallace Stevens." *Études Anglaises*, 12, 1959:222–30.

Bergler, E. "Psychoanalysis of Writers and Literary Productivity." In *Psychoanalysis and the Social Sciences*, Vol. 1, ed. G. Roheim. New York: International Universities Press, 1947, pp. 247–96.

Bibring, E. "The Mechanisms of Depression." In *Affective Disorders*, ed. P. Greenacre. New York: International Universities Press, 1953, pp. 13–48.

Biller, H. "Father Absence and the Personality Development of the Male Child." In *Annual Progress in Child Psychiatry and Child Development*, ed. S. Chess and A. Thomas. New York: Brunner/Mazel, 1971, pp. 120–52.

Bleich, D. "Emotional Origins of Literary Meaning." *College English*, 31, 1969:30–40.

Bleich, D. "The Subjective Paradigm in Science, Psychology, and Criticism." *New Literary History*, 7, 1975–76:313–34.

Blos, P. *On Adolescence: A Psychoanalytic Interpretation*. New York: Free Press, 1962.

163

Bonaparte, M. *The Life and Works of Edgar Allan Poe: A Psycho-Analytic Interpretation.* London: Imago, 1949.

Bose, A. "Some Poets of the Writers' Workshop." In *Critical Essays on Indian Writing in English: Presented to Armado Menezes*, ed. M. Naik, S. Desai, and G. Amur. Dharwar: Karnatak University Press, 1968, pp. 31–50.

Bowlby, J. *Attachment and Loss*, Vol. 1. New York: Basic Books, 1969.

Brazelton, T. and Stern, D. "Research in the Backgrounds of Psychotherapeutic Processes." Anniversary Conference of *The Psychoanalytic Review*, April 30, 1977.

Brooks, C. *The Well-Wrought Urn: Studies in the Structure of Poetry.* New York: Harcourt, Brace and World, 1947.

Burke, K. "Freud — and the Analysis of Poetry." *American Journal of Sociology*, 44, 1939.

Burnham, J. "Psychoanalysis and American Medicine 1894–1918: Medicine, Science, and Culture." *Psychological Issues*, Monograph No. 20. New York: International Universities Press, 1967.

Bush, M. "The Problem of Form in the Psychoanalytic Theory of Art." *Psychoanalytic Review*, 54, 1967:5–35.

Bychowski, G. "Metapsychology of Artistic Creation." *Psychoanalytic Quarterly*, 20, 1951:592–602.

Campbell, J. *The Hero with a Thousand Faces.* New York: World Publishing Company, 1949.

Chasseguet-Smirgel, J. "Feminine Guilt and the Oedipus Complex." In *Female Sexuality: New Psychoanalytic Views*, ed. J. Chasseguet-Smirgel. Ann Arbor: University of Michigan Press, 1970, pp. 94–134.

Cirlot, J. *A Dictionary of Symbols*, trans. J. Sage. New York: Philosophical Library, 1962.

Crews, F. *Sins of the Father: Hawthorne's Psychological Themes.* New York: Oxford University Press, 1966.

Crews, F. "Anesthetic Criticism." In *Psychoanalysis and Literary Process*, ed. F. Crews. Cambridge, Mass.: Winthrop, 1970, pp. 1–24.

Crews, F. "Reductionism and Its Discontents." *Critical Inquiry*, 1, 1975:543–58.

Daiches, D. *Critical Approaches to Literature.* New York: W. W. Norton, 1956.

Doggett, F. *Stevens' Poetry of Thought.* Baltimore: Johns-Hopkins University Press, 1966.

Dorpat, T. "Structural Conflict and Object Relations Conflict." *Journal of the American Psychoanalytic Association*, 24 (4), 1976:855–74.

Doubrovsky, S. " 'The Nine of Hearts': Fragment of a Psychoreading of *La Nausée.*" In *Psychoanalysis, Creativity, and Literature,* ed. A. Roland. New York: Columbia University Press, 1978, pp. 312–22.

Eissler, K. *Medical Orthodoxy and the Future of Psychoanalysis.* New York: International Universities Press, 1965.

Erikson, E. *Childhood and Society.* New York: W. W. Norton, 1950.

Erikson, E. *Identity: Youth and Crisis.* New York: W. W. Norton, 1968.

Erikson, E. *Gandhi's Truth: On the Origins of Militant Nonviolence.* New York: W. W. Norton, 1969.

Fairbairn, W. "The Ultimate Basis of Aesthetic Experience." *British Journal of Psychology,* 29, 1938:168–81.

Fenichel, O. *The Psychoanalytic Theory of Neurosis.* New York: W. W. Norton, 1945.

Fisher, S. and Greenberg, R. *The Scientific Credibility of Freud's Theories and Therapy.* New York: Basic Books, 1977.

Freud, S. and Breuer, J. *Studies in Hysteria* (1895). *Standard Edition of the Complete Psychological Works of Sigmund Freud,* 2, ed. J. Strachey. London: Hogarth Press, 1955, pp. 1–305.

Freud, S. *The Interpretation of Dreams* (1900). *Standard Edition of the Complete Psychological Works of Sigmund Freud,* 4–5, ed. J. Strachey. London: Hogarth Press, 1953, pp. 1–621.

Freud, S. *Jokes and their Relation to the Unconscious* (1905). *Standard Edition of the Complete Psychological Works of Sigmund Freud,* 8, ed. J. Strachey. London: Hogarth Press, 1960, pp. 9–236.

Freud, S. *Delusions and Dreams in Jensen's Gradiva* (1907). *Standard Edition of the Complete Psychological Works of Sigmund Freud,* 9, ed. J. Strachey. London: Hogarth Press, 1959, pp. 7–95.

Freud, S. "Creative Writers and Day-dreaming" (1908). In *Standard Edition of the Complete Psychological Works of Sigmund Freud,* 9, ed. J. Strachey. London: Hogarth Press, 1959, pp. 141–53.

Freud, S. "Analysis of a Phobia in a Five-Year-Old Boy" (1909). In *Standard Edition of the Complete Psychological Works of Sigmund Freud,* 10, ed. J. Strachey. London: Hogarth Press, 1955, pp. 5–149.

Freud, S. *Leonardo da Vinci and a Memory of his Childhood* (1910). *Standard Edition of the Complete Psychological Works of Sigmund Freud,* 11, ed. J. Strachey. London: Hogarth Press, 1957, pp. 59–137.

Freud, S. "The Theme of the Three Caskets" (1913a). In *Standard Edition of the Complete Psychological Works of Sigmund Freud,* 12, ed. J. Strachey. London: Hogarth Press, 1958, pp. 289–301.

Freud, S. *Totem and Taboo* (1913b). *Standard Edition of the Complete Psychological Works of Sigmund Freud*, 13, ed. J. Strachey. London: Hogarth Press, 1953, pp. 1–162.

Freud, S. "Mourning and Melancholia" (1917). In *Standard Edition of the Complete Psychological Works of Sigmund Freud*, 14, ed. J. Strachey. London: Hogarth Press, 1957, pp. 243–58.

Freud, S. " 'A Child Is Being Beaten': A Contribution to the Study of the Origin of Sexual Perversions" (1919). In *Standard Edition of the Complete Works of Sigmund Freud*, 17, ed. J. Strachey. London: Hogarth Press, 1955, pp. 179–204.

Fry, R. *The Artist and Psychoanalysis*. London: Hogarth Press, 1924.

Gill, M. "Metapsychology Is Not Psychology." In *Psychology Versus Metapsychology*, ed. M. Gill and P. Holzman. New York: International Universities Press, 1976, pp. 75–105.

Gray, P. "Theory and Evidence in Imprinting in Human Infants." *Journal of Psychology*, 46, 1958:155–166.

Green, A. "The Analyst, Symbolization and Absence in the Analytic Setting (On Changes in Analytic Practice and Analytic Experience)." *International Journal of Psycho-Analysis*, 56 (1), 1975: 1–22.

Griffin, W. "The Use and Abuse of Psychoanalysis in the Study of Literature." *Literature and Psychology*, 1, 1951:3–20.

Guntrip, H. *Psychoanalytic Theory, Therapy, and the Self*. New York: Basic Books, 1971.

Gutheil, E. *The Handbook of Dream Analysis*. New York: Washington Square Press, 1951.

Hamilton, J. "Transitional Fantasies and the Creative Process." In *The Psychoanalytic Study of Society*, Vol. 6, ed. W. Muensterberger and A. Esman. New York: International Universities Press, 1975, pp. 53–76.

Harrison, S. "Is Psychoanalysis 'Our Science'?: Reflections on the Scientific Status of Psychoanalysis." *Journal of the American Psychoanalytic Association*, 18, 1970, 125–49.

Hartmann, H. *Ego Psychology and the Problem of Adaptation*, trans. D. Rapaport. New York: International Universities Press, 1958, 1939.

Hartmann, H., Kris, E., and Loewenstein, R. "Notes on the Theory of Aggression." *Psychoanalytic Study of the Child*, 3–4, 1949, pp. 9–34.

Henry, N. "Dickinson's 'As By the Dead We Love to Sit.' " *The Explicator*, 31 (5) 1973, Item 35.

Hoffman, D. *Poe Poe Poe Poe Poe Poe Poe*. New York: Doubleday, 1972.

Hoffman, F. *Freudianism and the Literary Mind*. Baton Rouge: Louisiana State University Press, 1945.

Holland, N. "Shakespearean Tragedy and the Three Ways of Psychoanalytic Criticism." *The Hudson Review*, 15(2), 1962, 217–27.

Holland, N. *The Dynamics of Literary Response*. New York: Oxford University Press, 1968.

Holland, N. *Poems in Persons: An Introduction to the Psychoanalysis of Literature*. New York: W. W. Norton, 1973(a).

Holland, N. "A Letter to Leonard." *Hartford Studies in Literature*, 5 (Triple issue), 1973:9–30.

Holland, N. *Five Readers Reading*. New Haven: Yale University Press, 1975(a).

Holland, N. "Unity Identity Text Self." *Publication of the Modern Language Association*, 90(5) 1975b:813–22.

Holland, N. "What Can a Concept of Identity Add to Psycholinguistics?" *Psychiatry and the Humanities*, 3, 1978.

Horner, A. "Stages and Processes in the Development of Early Object Relations and Their Associated Pathologies." *International Review of Psycho-Analysis*, 2, 1975:95–105.

Horney, K. *Feminine Psychology*. New York: W. W. Norton, 1967.

Jacobson, E. *The Self and the Object World*. New York: International Universities Press, 1964.

Jacobson, E. "Problems in the Differentiation Between Schizophrenic and Melancholic States of Depression." In *Psychoanalysis — A General Psychology*, ed. R. Loewenstein, L. Newman, M. Schur, and A. Solnit. New York: International Universities Press, 1966, pp. 499–518.

James, H. *The Portrait of a Lady*. Boston: Houghton Mifflin Co., 1963.

Jones, E. *Hamlet and Oedipus*. New York: Doubleday, 1955.

Jung, C. "On the Relation of Analytical Psychology to Poetry" (1922). In *The Collected Works of Carl G. Jung*, 15, trans. R. Hull. Princeton: Princeton University Press, 1966, pp. 65–83.

Jung, C. "Psychology and Literature" (1930). In *The Collected Works of Carl G. Jung*, 15, trans. R. Hull. Princeton: Princeton University Press, 1966, pp. 84–105.

Jung, C. "The Difference Between Eastern and Western Thinking" (1939). In *The Collected Works of Carl G. Jung*, 11, trans. R. Hull. Princeton: Princeton University Press, 1958, pp. 475–93.

Jung, C. "The Undiscovered Self (Present and Future)" (1957). In *The Collected Works of Carl G. Jung*, 10, trans. R. Hull. Princeton: Princeton University Press, 1964, pp. 245–305.

Kakar, S. *The Inner World: A Psycho-analytic Study of Childhood and Society in India*. New York: Oxford University Press, 1978.

Kaplan, M. and Kloss, R. *The Unspoken Motive: A Guide to Psychoanalytic Literary Criticism*. New York: Free Press, 1973.

Kazin, A. "Psychoanalysis and Literary Culture Today" (1959). In *Psychoanalysis and Literature*, ed. H. Ruitenbeek. New York: Dutton, 1964, 3–13.

Kernberg, O. *Borderline Conditions and Pathological Narcissism*. New York: Jason Aronson, 1975.

Kernberg, O. *Object Relations Theory and Clinical Psychoanalysis*. New York: Jason Aronson, 1976.

Kessler, E. *Images of Wallace Stevens*. New Brunswick: Rutgers University Press, 1972.

Kestenberg, J. *Children and Parents: Psychoanalytic Studies in Development*. New York: Jason Aronson, 1975.

Kline, N. *Fact and Fantasy in Freudian Theory*. London: Methuen, 1972.

Kohut, H. *The Restoration of the Self*. New York: International Universities Press, 1977.

Kris, E. *Psychoanalytic Explorations in Art*. New York: Schocken Books, 1952.

Kris, E. "Psychoanalysis and the Study of Creative Imagination." *Bulletin of the New York Academy of Medicine*, 29, 1953:334–51.

Kubie, L. *Neurotic Distortion of the Creative Process*. New York: Noonday Press, 1958.

Kuhn, T. *The Structure of Scientific Revolutions*. Chicago: University of Chicago Press, 1962.

Lacan, J. *Ecrits*. Paris: Le Seuil, 1966.

Lagache, D. (1955) *La Psychoanalyse*. Paris: Presses Universitaires de France, 1955.

Lagache, D. "Psychoanalysis as an Exact Science." In *Psychoanalysis — A General Psychology*, ed. R. Loewenstein, L. Newman, M. Schur, and A. Solnit. New York: International Universities Press, 1966, pp. 400–434.

Lavers, A. "The World as Icon: On Sylvia Plath's Themes." In *The Art of Sylvia Plath: A Symposium*, ed. C. Newman. London: Faber, 1970, pp. 100–135.

Lesser, S. *Fiction and the Unconscious*. Boston: Beacon Press, 1957.

Lichtenstein, H. "Identity and Sexuality: A Study of Their Interrelationship in Man." *Journal of the American Psychoanalytic Association*, 9, 1961, pp. 179–260.

Lidz, T. *The Person*. New York: Basic Books, 1968.

Lucie-Smith, E. "Sea-Imagery in the Work of Sylvia Plath." In *The Art of Sylvia Plath: A Symposium*, ed. C. Newman. London: Faber, 1970, pp. 91–99.

Mahler, M. *On Human Symbiosis and the Vicissitudes of Individuation*. New York: International Universities Press, 1968.

Mahler, M. Pine, F., and Bergmann, A. *The Psychological Birth of the Human Infant: Symbiosis and Individuation*. New York: Basic Books, 1975.

Mayman, M. "Psychoanalytic Theory in Retrospect and Prospect." *Bulletin of the Menninger Clinic*, 40(3), 1976, pp. 199–210.

McCurdy, H. "Review of *The Design Within: Psychoanalytic Approaches to Shakespeare*, ed. M. Faber." *Contemporary Psychology*, 16, 1971:115–17.

Meissner, W. "Some Notes on the Psychology of the Literary Character: A Psychoanalytic Perspective." *Seminars in Psychiatry*, 5 (3), 1973:261–74.

Meissner, W. "New Horizons in Metapsychology: View and Review." *Journal of the American Psychoanalytic Association*, 24(1) 1976:161–80.

Miel, J. "Jacques Lacan and the Structure of the Unconscious." (1965). In *Structuralism*, ed. J. Ehrmann. New York: Anchor, 1970, pp. 94–101.

Miller, E. *Melville*. New York: George Braziller, Inc., 1975.

Miller, J. *Psychoanalysis and Women: Contributions to New Theory and Therapy*. New York: Brunner/Mazel, 1973.

Miller, J. *Toward a New Psychology of Women*. Boston: Beacon Press, 1976.

Modell, A. *Object Love and Reality*. New York: International Universities Press, 1968.

Modell, A. "The Transitional Object and the Creative Act." *Psychoanalytic Quarterly*, 39, 1970:240–50.

Mollinger, R. "Dom Moraes' Vision: From Dream to Nightmare." *Creative Moment*, 3(2), 1974:5–11.

Mollinger, R. "Sylvia Plath's 'Private Ground.' " *Notes on Contemporary Literature*, 5(2) 1975:14–15.

Mollinger, R. "Wallace Stevens' Search for the Central Man." *Tennessee Studies in Literature*, 21, 1976:66–79.

Mollinger, R. "The Lay Analyst as Humanist." *The Psychocultural Review*, 1(1), 1977:112–13.

Mollinger, R. and Mollinger, S. "Edgar Allan Poe's 'The Oval Portrait.' " *American Imago*, 36(2), 1979:147–53.

Mollinger, S. "Hawthorne, Language, and Reality." Unpublished dissertation, Columbia University, 1978.

Moraes, D. *A Beginning*. London: Parton Press, rev. ed. 1958.

Moraes, D. *Poems*. London: Eyre and Spottiswoode, 1960.

Moraes, D. *John Nobody*. London: Eyre and Spottiswoode, 1965(a).

Moraes, D. *Poems 1955–1965*. New York: Macmillan, 1965(b).

Morrison, C. *Freud and the Critic: The Early Use of Depth Psychology in Literary Criticism*. Chapel Hill: University of North Carolina Press, 1968.

Mullahy, P. *Oedipus: Myth and Complex*. New York: Grove Press, 1948.

Müller-Braunschweig, H. *The Psychoanalytic Study of Society*, Vol. 6, ed. W. Muensterberger and A. Esman. New York: International Universities Press, 1975.

Murray, H. "Bartleby and I." A Symposium: "Bartleby the Scrivener," ed. P. Howard. *Melville Annual*, 1965:3–24.

Nandy, P. "Indian Poetry in English: The Dynamics of a New Sensibility." *Indian Literature*, 14, 1974:9–18.

Neumann, E. *Art and the Creative Unconscious*. Princeton: Princeton University Press, 1959.

Noland, R. "The Future of Psychological Criticism." *Hartford Studies in Literature*, 5 (Triple Issue), 1973:88–105.

Noy, P. "A Theory of Art and Aesthetic Experience." *Psychoanalytic Review*, 55, 1969:623–45.

Orgel, S. "Sylvia Plath: Fusion with the Victim and Suicide." *Psychoanalytic Quarterly*, 43, 1974:262–87.

Plath, S. *The Colossus and Other Poems*. New York: Alfred Knopf, 1957.

Plath, S. *Ariel*. New York: Harper and Row, 1966.

Plath, S. *Crossing the Water*. New York: Harper and Row, 1971.

Poe, E. "The Fall of the House of Usher." *Tales of Mystery and Imagination*. New York: Dutton, 1971, pp. 128–44.

Pope, A. "Essay on Man." In *The Poetry of Pope: A Selection*, ed. M. H. Abrams. New York: Appleton-Century-Crofts, 1954, pp. 49–81.

Prescott, F. *Poetry and Dreams*. Boston: The Four Seas Company, 1912.

Quinn, P. *The French Face of Edgar Poe*. Carbondale: Southern Illinois University Press, 1957.

Rank, O. "The Myth of the Birth of the Hero: A Psychological Interpretation of Mythology." In *The Myth of the Birth of the Hero and Other Writings*, ed. P. Freund. New York: Vintage, 1959, pp. 1–96.

Rapaport, D. and Gill, M. "The Points of View and Assumptions of Metapsychology." *International Journal of Psycho-Analysis*, 40, 1959:153–62.

Ricoeur, P. "Psychoanalysis and the Work of Art." In *Psychiatry and the Humanities*, Vol. 1, ed. J. Smith. New Haven: Yale University Press, 1976, pp. 3–33.

Roland, A. "Towards a Reorientation of Psychoanalytic Literary Criticism." In *Psychoanalysis, Creativity, and Literature: A French-American Inquiry*, ed. A. Roland. New York: Columbia University Press, 1978, pp. 248–70.

Roland, A. and Rizzo, G. "Psychoanalysis in Search of Pirandello: *Six Characters* and *Henry IV*." *Psychoanalytic Review*, 64 (1), 1977:63–99.

Rose, G. "Fusion States." In *Tactics and Techniques in Psychoanalytic Therapy*, Vol. 1, ed. P. Giovacchini. New York: Jason Aronson, 1972, pp. 170–88.

Rothenberg, A. "The Defense of Psychoanalysis in Literature." *Comparative Drama*, 7, 1973:51–67.

Rothenberg, A. "Homospatial Thinking in Creativity." *Archives of General Psychiatry*, 33, 1976:17–26.

Rothenberg, A. "The Unconscious and Creativity." In *Creativity and Literature: A French-American Inquiry*, ed. A. Roland. New York: Columbia University Press, 1978, pp. 144–61.

Rycroft, C. *Imagination and Reality*. New York: International Universities Press, 1968.

Schafer, R. *A New Language for Psychoanalysis*. New Haven: Yale University Press, 1976.

Schuyler, D. *The Depressive Spectrum*. New York: Jason Aronson, 1974.

Schwartz, M. "Introduction: The Space in Psychological Criticism." *Hartford Studies in Literature*, 5(Triple issue), 1973:x–xxi.

Schwartz, M. "Where Is Literature?" *College English*, 36(7), 1975:756–65.

Slochower, H. "The Psychoanalytic Approach to Literature: Some Pitfalls and Promises." *Literature and Psychology*, 21, 1971:107–11.

Smirnoff, V. *The Scope of Child Analysis*. New York: International Universities Press, 1971.

Snider, C. "C. G. Jung's Analytical Psychology and Literary Criticism." *Psychocultural Review*, 1(1), 1977:99–108(a).

Snider, C. "Jung's Psychology of the Conscious and the Unconscious." *Psychocultural Review*, 1(2), 1977:216–42(b).

Spitz, R. *No and Yes: On the Genesis of Human Communication*. New York: International Universities Press, 1957.

Spitz, R. *The First Year of Life*. New York: International Universities Press, 1965.

Spitz, R. "Metapsychology and Direct Infant Observation." In *Psychoanalysis — A General Psychology*, R. Loewenstein, L. Newman, M. Schur, and A. Solnit. New York: International Universities Press, 1966, pp. 123–51.

Stekel, W. "Poetry and Neurosis," trans. J. Van Teslaar. *Psychoanalytic Review*, 10, 1923:73–93.

Stevens, W. *Parts of a World*. New York: Alfred Knopf, 1942.

Stevens, W. *The Necessary Angel: Essays on Reality and the Imagination*. New York: Alfred Knopf, 1951.

Stevens, W. *The Collected Poems of Wallace Stevens*. New York: Alfred Knopf, 1954.

Stevens, W. *Opus Posthumous*. New York: Alfred Knopf, 1969 (1957).

Stevens, W. *Letters of Wallace Stevens*, ed. H. Stevens. New York: Alfred Knopf, 1966.

Sukenick, R. *Wallace Stevens: Musing the Obscure*. New York: New York University Press, 1967.

Thackaberry, R. and Lash, K. "Stevens' 'The Emperor of Ice-Cream.' " *The Explicator*, 6(6), 1948, Item 36.

Torok, M. "The Significance of Penis Envy in Women." *Female Sexuality: New Psychoanalytic Views*, ed. J. Chasseguet-Smirgel. Ann Arbor: University of Michigan Press, 1970, pp. 135–70.

Trilling, L. "Freud and Literature" (1940). *The Liberal Imagination*. New York: Viking, 1950, pp. 44–64.

Trilling, L. "Art and Neurosis" (1945). *The Liberal Imagination*. New York: Viking, 1950, pp. 159–78.

Waldoff, L. "Perceiving and Creating in Literature." *Hartford Studies in Literature*, 7, 1975:154–69.

Wallerstein, R. "Psychoanalysis as a Science: Its Present Status and Its Future Tasks." In *Psychology Versus Metapsychology*, ed. M. Gill and P. Holzman. New York: International Universities Press, 1976, pp. 198–228.

Weil, A. "The First Year: Metapsychological Inferences of Infant Observation." In *The Process of Child Development*, ed. P. Neubauer. New York: New American Library, 1976, pp. 246–65.

Weissman, P. "Psychological Concomitants of Ego Functions in Creativity." *International Journal of Psycho-Analysis*, 49, 1968:464–69.

Wilson, E. *The Wound and the Bow*. New York: Houghton Mifflin, 1941.

Winnicott, D. "The Manic Defense" (1935). *Collected Papers: Through Paediatrics to Psychoanalysis*. New York: Basic Books, 1958, pp. 129–44.

Winnicott, D. "Transitional Objects and Transitional Phenomena" (1951). *Collected Papers: Through Paediatrics to Psychoanalysis*. New York: Basic Books, 1958, pp. 229–42.

Winnicott, D. "Ego Distortion in Terms of True and False Self" (1960). In *The Maturational Processes and the Facilitating Environment*. New York: International Universities Press, 1965, pp. 140–52.

Winnicott, D. "Communicating and Not Communicating Leading to a Study of Certain Opposites" (1963). *The Maturational Processes and the Facilitating Environment*. New York: International Universities Press, 1965, pp. 179–92.

Winnicott, D. "The Location of Cultural Experience" (1967). *Playing and Reality*, New York: Basic Books, 1971, pp. 95–103.

Winnicott, D. *Playing and Reality*. New York: Basic Books, 1971.

Young, P. "The Earlier Psychologists and Poe." *American Literature*, 22, 1951:44–54.

# Index

175